Learning about Multiplication

W9-BMW-870

Multiplication is a short way to add groups of equal size.

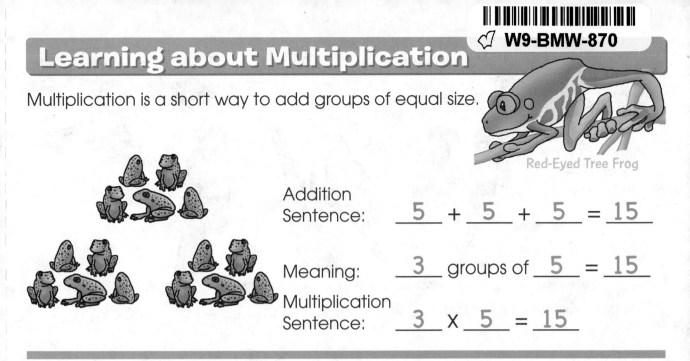

Red-Eyed Tree Frog

Addition Sentence: __5__ + __5__ + __5__ = __15__

Meaning: __3__ groups of __5__ = __15__

Multiplication Sentence: __3__ X __5__ = __15__

Write addition and multiplication sentences to tell how many there are.

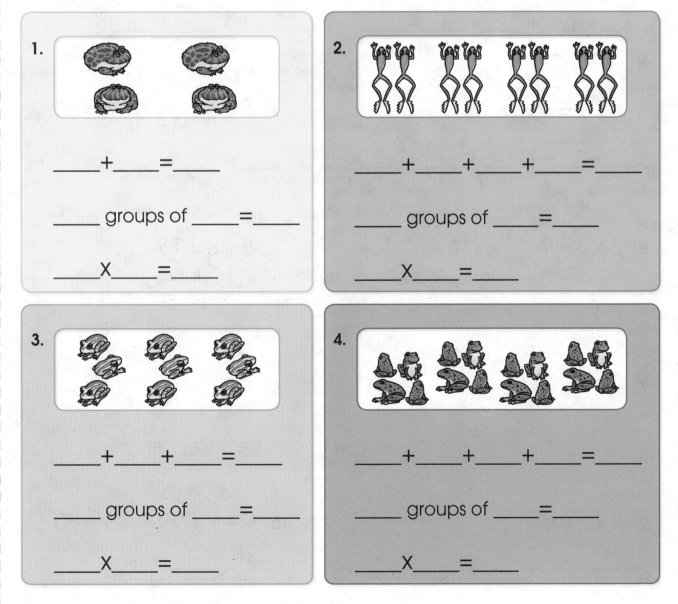

1.

____+____=____

____ groups of ____=____

____X____=____

2.

____+____+____+____=____

____ groups of ____=____

____X____=____

3.

____+____+____=____

____ groups of ____=____

____X____=____

4.

____+____+____+____=____

____ groups of ____=____

____X____=____

Learning about Multiplication

Multiplication is the same as repeated addition.

$2 + 2 + 2 = 6$
$3 \times 2 = 6$

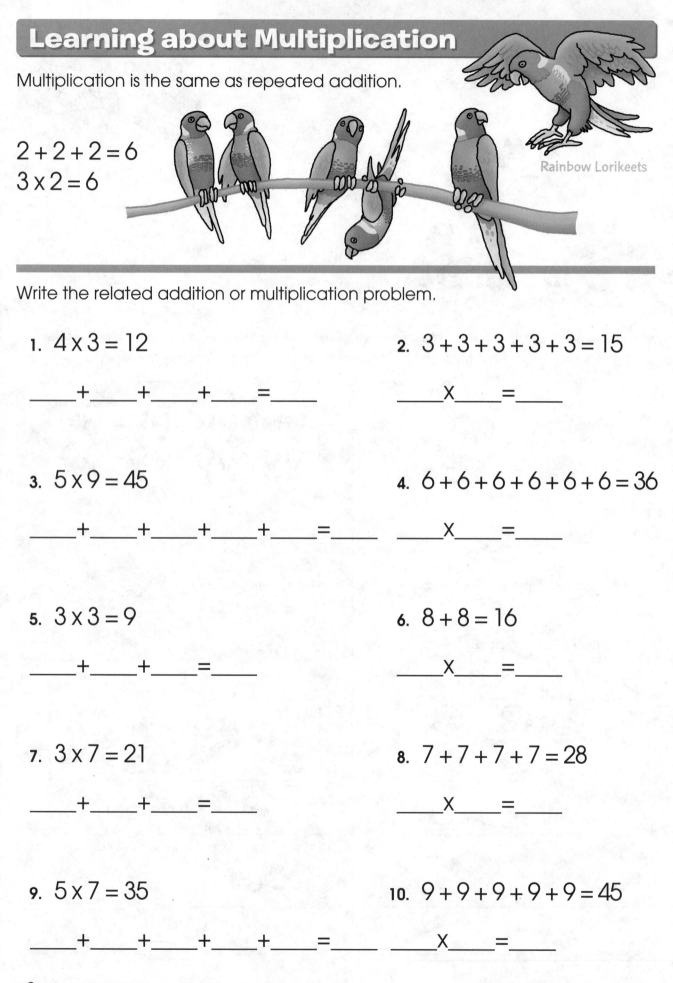

Rainbow Lorikeets

Write the related addition or multiplication problem.

1. $4 \times 3 = 12$

____ + ____ + ____ + ____ = ____

2. $3 + 3 + 3 + 3 + 3 = 15$

____ X ____ = ____

3. $5 \times 9 = 45$

____ + ____ + ____ + ____ + ____ = ____

4. $6 + 6 + 6 + 6 + 6 + 6 = 36$

____ X ____ = ____

5. $3 \times 3 = 9$

____ + ____ + ____ = ____

6. $8 + 8 = 16$

____ X ____ = ____

7. $3 \times 7 = 21$

____ + ____ + ____ = ____

8. $7 + 7 + 7 + 7 = 28$

____ X ____ = ____

9. $5 \times 7 = 35$

____ + ____ + ____ + ____ + ____ = ____

10. $9 + 9 + 9 + 9 + 9 = 45$

____ X ____ = ____

© School Zone Publishing Company 02215

Learning about Multiplication

2 groups
3 in each group
2 x 3 = 6

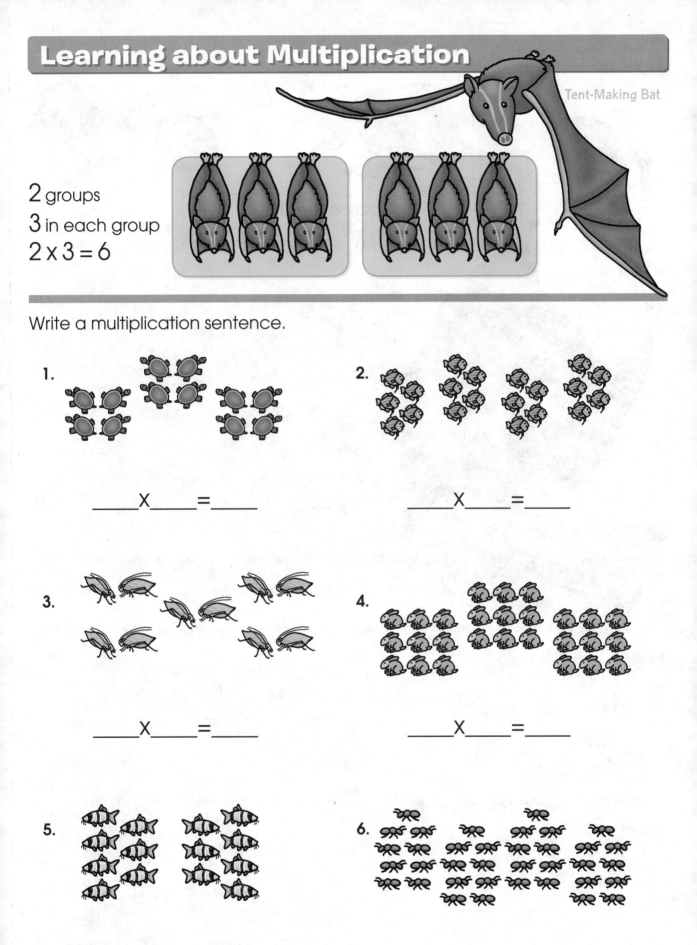

Write a multiplication sentence.

1.

_____X_____=_____

2.

_____X_____=_____

3.

_____X_____=_____

4.

_____X_____=_____

5.

_____X_____=_____

6.

_____X_____=_____

Multiplication Facts: 2s and 3s

Practice the facts.

1. 2 x 1 = ____
   2 x 2 = ____
   2 x 3 = ____
   2 x 4 = ____
   2 x 5 = ____
   2 x 6 = ____
   2 x 7 = ____
   2 x 8 = ____
   2 x 9 = ____

Count by 2s to check your answers.

2. 3 x 1 = ____
   3 x 2 = ____
   3 x 3 = ____
   3 x 4 = ____
   3 x 5 = ____
   3 x 6 = ____
   3 x 7 = ____
   3 x 8 = ____
   3 x 9 = ____

Count by 3s to check your answers.

Toucan

If you change the order of the factors, the product is the same.

2 groups of 3   3 groups of 2

2 x 3 = 6   3 x 2 = 6
↑   ↑   ↑
factors product

This is the **commutative property** of multiplication.

Multiply.

3. 2 x 4 = ____   4 x 2 = ____

4. 3 x 6 = ____   6 x 3 = ____

5. 3 x 4 = ____   4 x 3 = ____

6. 7 x 2 = ____   2 x 7 = ____

7. 2 x 3 = ____   3 x 2 = ____

   © School Zone Publishing Company 02215

Practice the facts.

1. $4 \times 1 = \rule{1cm}{0.4pt}$
   $4 \times 2 = \rule{1cm}{0.4pt}$
   $4 \times 3 = \rule{1cm}{0.4pt}$
   $4 \times 4 = \rule{1cm}{0.4pt}$
   $4 \times 5 = \rule{1cm}{0.4pt}$
   $4 \times 6 = \rule{1cm}{0.4pt}$
   $4 \times 7 = \rule{1cm}{0.4pt}$
   $4 \times 8 = \rule{1cm}{0.4pt}$
   $4 \times 9 = \rule{1cm}{0.4pt}$

Count by 4s to check your answers.

2. $5 \times 1 = \rule{1cm}{0.4pt}$
   $5 \times 2 = \rule{1cm}{0.4pt}$
   $5 \times 3 = \rule{1cm}{0.4pt}$
   $5 \times 4 = \rule{1cm}{0.4pt}$
   $5 \times 5 = \rule{1cm}{0.4pt}$
   $5 \times 6 = \rule{1cm}{0.4pt}$
   $5 \times 7 = \rule{1cm}{0.4pt}$
   $5 \times 8 = \rule{1cm}{0.4pt}$
   $5 \times 9 = \rule{1cm}{0.4pt}$

Count by 5s to check your answers.

The ones digit is
$\rule{1cm}{0.4pt}$ or $\rule{1cm}{0.4pt}$.

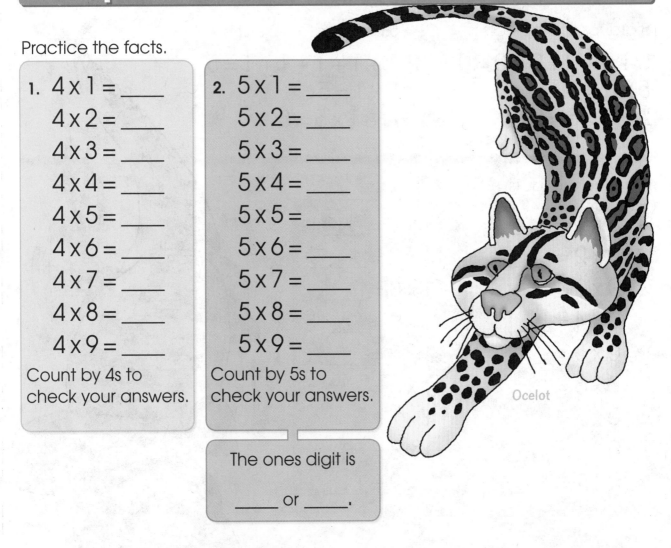

Ocelot

Draw groups of objects to show each multiplication fact.

3. $4 \times 3 = 12$

4. $5 \times 4 = 20$

5. $4 \times 7 = 28$

6. $5 \times 6 = 30$

7. $5 \times 1 = 5$

8. $5 \times 3 = 15$

Multiplication Facts: 0s and 1s

5 groups of 0 objects is

$0 + 0 + 0 + 0 + 0 = 0$
$5 \times 0 = 0$
And $0 \times 5 = 0$

5 groups of 1 object is

$1 + 1 + 1 + 1 + 1 = 5$
$5 \times 1 = 5$
And $1 \times 5 = 5$

Practice the facts.

1. $0 \times 1 =$ _____
    $0 \times 2 =$ _____
    $0 \times 3 =$ _____
    $0 \times 4 =$ _____
    $0 \times 5 =$ _____
    $0 \times 6 =$ _____
    $0 \times 7 =$ _____
    $0 \times 8 =$ _____
    $0 \times 9 =$ _____

2. $1 \times 1 =$ _____
    $1 \times 2 =$ _____
    $1 \times 3 =$ _____
    $1 \times 4 =$ _____
    $1 \times 5 =$ _____
    $1 \times 6 =$ _____
    $1 \times 7 =$ _____
    $1 \times 8 =$ _____
    $1 \times 9 =$ _____

Spectacled Caiman

3. Look at all the products in problem 1. What is the product of 0 and any number? _____

    This is the **zero property** of multiplication.

4. Look at all the products in problem 2. What is the product of 1 and any number? _____

    This is the **identity property** of multiplication.

    © School Zone Publishing Company 02215

Multiplication Facts Review

1. Fill in the table. Look for patterns in the table.

x	0	1	2	3	4	5	6	7	8	9
0									0	
1										9
2							12			
3										
4		4								
5	0		10							

Harpy Eagle

2. Look at the 2s row. List the products. _____

   What are the ones digits of the 2s facts? _____

3. Look at the 5s row. List the products. _____

   What are the ones digits of the 5s facts? _____

4. Look at the 1s row. What do you notice about the products?_____

   _____

5. Look at the 0s row. What is each product? _____
   Also, remember that 0 x 0 = 0.

6. What is 3 x 5? _____   What is 5 x 3? _____

   What is 3 x 2? _____   What is 2 x 3? _____

   Why are the products the same for each pair of facts? _____

   _____

Practice the facts.

1. 6 x 0 = ____
   6 x 1 = ____
   6 x 2 = ____
   6 x 3 = ____
   6 x 4 = ____
   6 x 5 = ____
   6 x 6 = ____
   6 x 7 = ____
   6 x 8 = ____
   6 x 9 = ____

   Count by 6s to check your answers.

2. 7 x 0 = ____
   7 x 1 = ____
   7 x 2 = ____
   7 x 3 = ____
   7 x 4 = ____
   7 x 5 = ____
   7 x 6 = ____
   7 x 7 = ____
   7 x 8 = ____
   7 x 9 = ____

   Count by 7s to check your answers.

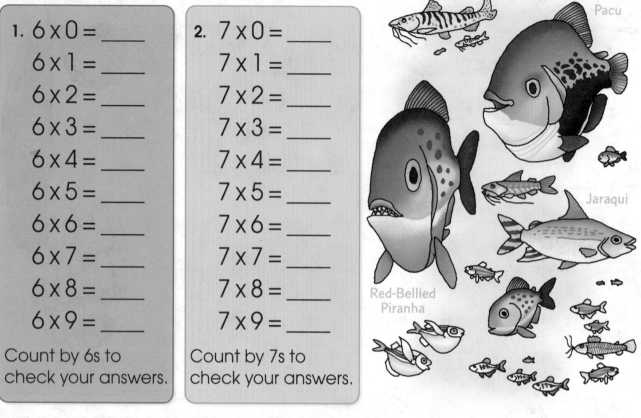

Pacu

Jaraqui

Red-Bellied Piranha

3. Find as many multiplication facts as you can in this number search puzzle.

7	5	35	5	8	40	3	2
3	6	18	3	1	3	2	4
21	30	42	15	8	5	6	8
7	9	63	4	6	24	9	7
8	7	56	3	48	6	4	2
7	8	49	12	54	28	36	4
7	1	7	5	35	6	0	0

Hint: There are 10 facts across, 9 facts down, and 9 facts along the diagonal. List the 28 facts on another sheet of paper.

Surubim

© School Zone Publishing Company 02215

Multiplication Facts: 8s and 9s

If you know your 4s facts, you can double them to know the 8s facts.

$4 \times 3 = 12$
$4 \times 3 = 12$
↓   ↓   ↓
$8 \times 3 = 24$

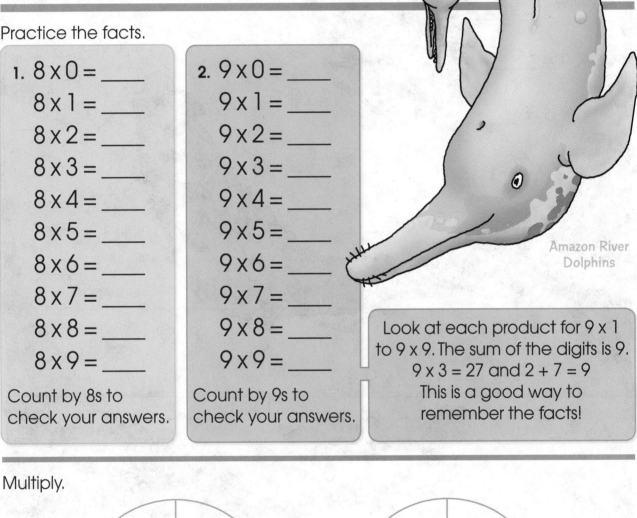

Amazon River Dolphins

Practice the facts.

1. $8 \times 0 =$ _____
    $8 \times 1 =$ _____
    $8 \times 2 =$ _____
    $8 \times 3 =$ _____
    $8 \times 4 =$ _____
    $8 \times 5 =$ _____
    $8 \times 6 =$ _____
    $8 \times 7 =$ _____
    $8 \times 8 =$ _____
    $8 \times 9 =$ _____

Count by 8s to check your answers.

2. $9 \times 0 =$ _____
    $9 \times 1 =$ _____
    $9 \times 2 =$ _____
    $9 \times 3 =$ _____
    $9 \times 4 =$ _____
    $9 \times 5 =$ _____
    $9 \times 6 =$ _____
    $9 \times 7 =$ _____
    $9 \times 8 =$ _____
    $9 \times 9 =$ _____

Count by 9s to check your answers.

Look at each product for 9 x 1 to 9 x 9. The sum of the digits is 9.
$9 \times 3 = 27$ and $2 + 7 = 9$
This is a good way to remember the facts!

Multiply.

3.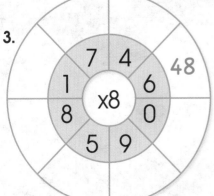

4.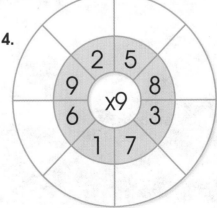

Multiplication Facts Review

Time yourself. How many minutes will it take you to go from the waterfall to the village? Call out the answers to a friend. Can you do it in less than 3 minutes? Practice until you can do the whole thing in less than 1 minute!

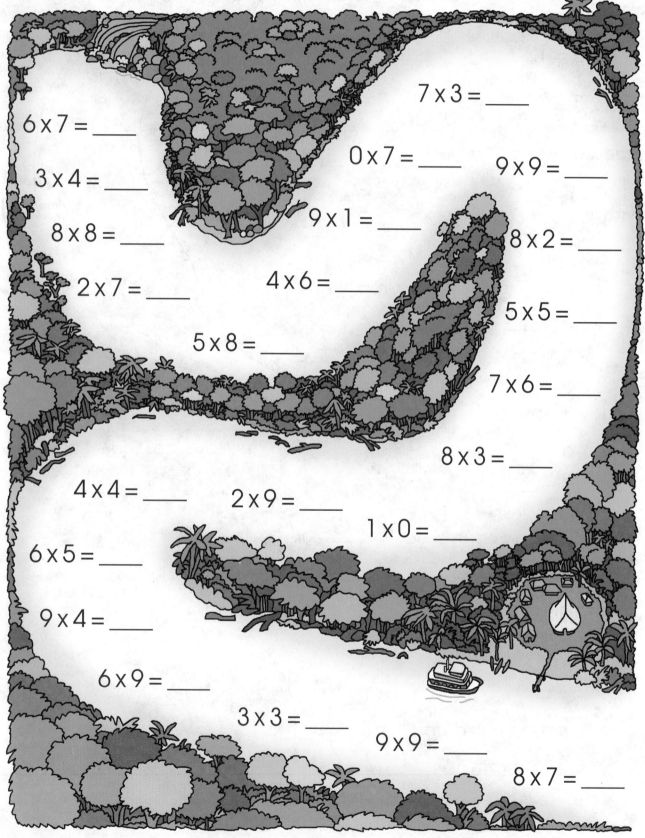

6 x 7 = ____

3 x 4 = ____

8 x 8 = ____

2 x 7 = ____

7 x 3 = ____

0 x 7 = ____

9 x 1 = ____

4 x 6 = ____

5 x 8 = ____

9 x 9 = ____

8 x 2 = ____

5 x 5 = ____

7 x 6 = ____

8 x 3 = ____

4 x 4 = ____

2 x 9 = ____

1 x 0 = ____

6 x 5 = ____

9 x 4 = ____

6 x 9 = ____

3 x 3 = ____

9 x 9 = ____

8 x 7 = ____

© School Zone Publishing Company 02215

The "Find the Products" Game

The first player to get four in a row **wins**!

How to play:

1. You'll need 2 or more players.

2. Take turns calling out facts, such as 7 x 5.

3. Using a different color marker for each player, write your answer where the two numbers meet on the chart. Example: 7 x 5 = 35

4. Try to block your opponent from getting four in a row.

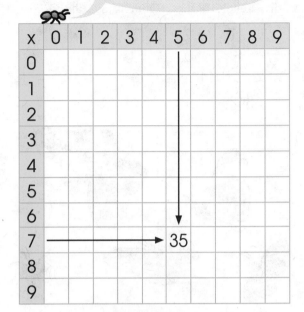

x	0	1	2	3	4	5	6	7	8	9
0										
1										
2										
3										
4										
5										
6										
7						35				
8										
9										

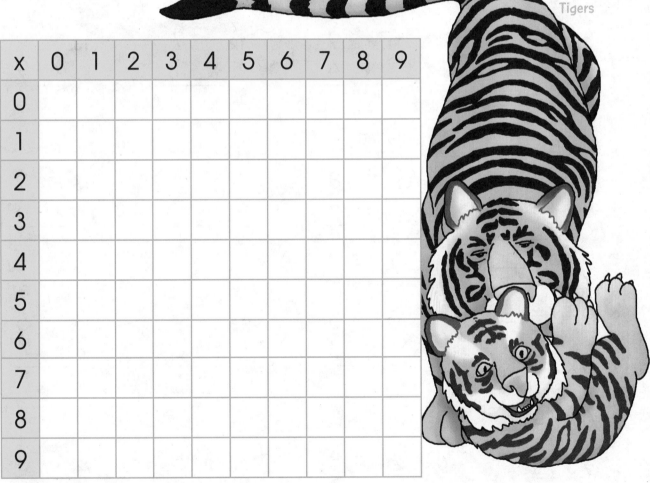

Tigers

x	0	1	2	3	4	5	6	7	8	9
0										
1										
2										
3										
4										
5										
6										
7										
8										
9										

Use this chart to check multiplication problems on other pages.

Writing Multiplication Facts Two Ways

Multiplication problems can be written two ways.

$$\begin{array}{r} 4 \\ \times\ \ 3 \\ \hline 12 \end{array}$$ is the same as $4 \times 3 = 12$.

Tithorea

Cattle Heart

Cyrbia

Scarce Bamboo

Tiger Mimic

Brown Siproeta

Red Rum

Orange Julia

Tailed Jay

Blue Morpho

Multiply.

1. $3 \times 2 = \underline{\hspace{1cm}}$

2. $3 \times 9 = \underline{\hspace{1cm}}$

3. $4 \times 5 = \underline{\hspace{1cm}}$

4. $4 \times 9 = \underline{\hspace{1cm}}$

5. $5 \times 6 = \underline{\hspace{1cm}}$

6. $5 \times 9 = \underline{\hspace{1cm}}$

7. $6 \times 2 = \underline{\hspace{1cm}}$

8. $6 \times 7 = \underline{\hspace{1cm}}$

9. $7 \times 4 = \underline{\hspace{1cm}}$

10. $7 \times 8 = \underline{\hspace{1cm}}$

11. $$\begin{array}{r} 9 \\ \times\ \ 4 \\ \hline \end{array}$$

12. $$\begin{array}{r} 7 \\ \times\ \ 1 \\ \hline \end{array}$$

13. $$\begin{array}{r} 9 \\ \times\ \ 9 \\ \hline \end{array}$$

14. $$\begin{array}{r} 8 \\ \times\ \ 5 \\ \hline \end{array}$$

15. $$\begin{array}{r} 8 \\ \times\ \ 7 \\ \hline \end{array}$$

16. $$\begin{array}{r} 9 \\ \times\ \ 8 \\ \hline \end{array}$$

17. $$\begin{array}{r} 5 \\ \times\ \ 3 \\ \hline \end{array}$$

18. $$\begin{array}{r} 9 \\ \times\ \ 6 \\ \hline \end{array}$$

19. $$\begin{array}{r} 5 \\ \times\ \ 4 \\ \hline \end{array}$$

20. $$\begin{array}{r} 8 \\ \times\ \ 4 \\ \hline \end{array}$$

21. $$\begin{array}{r} 5 \\ \times\ \ 0 \\ \hline \end{array}$$

22. $$\begin{array}{r} 6 \\ \times\ \ 6 \\ \hline \end{array}$$

© School Zone Publishing Company 02215

Finding Missing Factors

factor   factor   product

$5 \times \underline{\quad} = 35$

The missing factor is 7 because $5 \times 7 = 35$.

Common Iguana

Find the missing factor.

1. $5 \times \underline{\quad} = 20$

2. $9 \times \underline{\quad} = 63$

3. $9 \times \underline{\quad} = 9$

4. $5 \times \underline{\quad} = 40$

5. $\underline{\quad} \times 8 = 32$

6. $\underline{\quad} \times 4 = 24$

7. $9 \times \underline{\quad} = 81$

8. $6 \times \underline{\quad} = 42$

9. $\underline{\quad} \times 7 = 14$

10. $\underline{\quad} \times 7 = 49$

11. $\underline{\quad} \times 1 = 9$

12. $\underline{\quad} \times 1 = 0$

13. $3 \times \underline{\quad} = 0$

14. $9 \times \underline{\quad} = 72$

15. $4 \times \underline{\quad} = 12$

16. $8 \times \underline{\quad} = 64$

Caiman Lizard

Forest Iguana

Multiplying by 10

Find the amounts in cents.

1.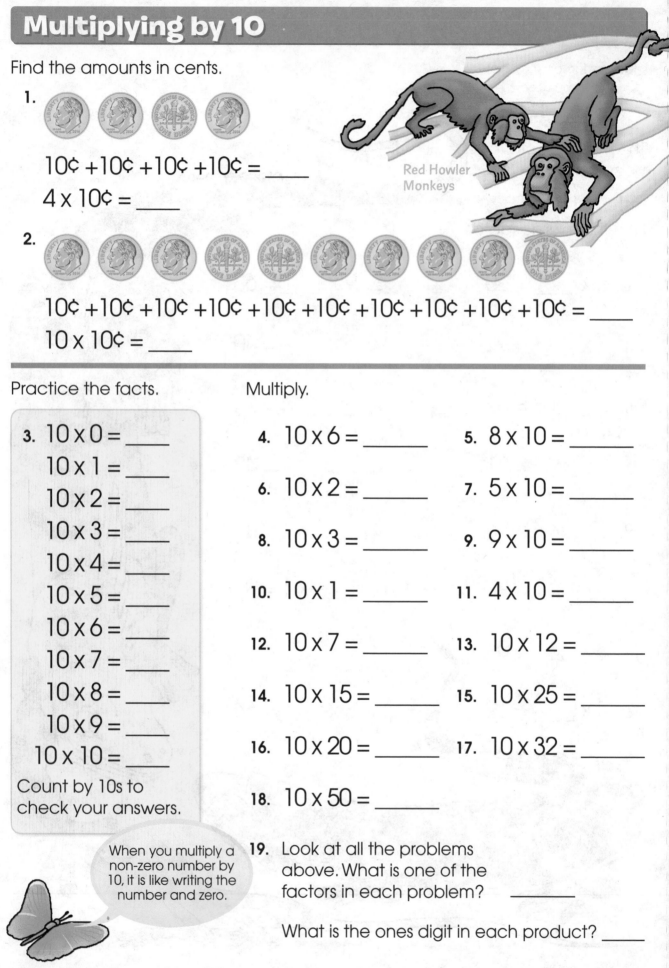

   $10¢ + 10¢ + 10¢ + 10¢ = $ ____

   $4 \times 10¢ = $ ____

   Red Howler Monkeys

2.

   $10¢ + 10¢ + 10¢ + 10¢ + 10¢ + 10¢ + 10¢ + 10¢ + 10¢ + 10¢ = $ ____

   $10 \times 10¢ = $ ____

Practice the facts.

3. $10 \times 0 = $ ____

   $10 \times 1 = $ ____

   $10 \times 2 = $ ____

   $10 \times 3 = $ ____

   $10 \times 4 = $ ____

   $10 \times 5 = $ ____

   $10 \times 6 = $ ____

   $10 \times 7 = $ ____

   $10 \times 8 = $ ____

   $10 \times 9 = $ ____

   $10 \times 10 = $ ____

Count by 10s to check your answers.

Multiply.

4. $10 \times 6 = $ _____

5. $8 \times 10 = $ _____

6. $10 \times 2 = $ _____

7. $5 \times 10 = $ _____

8. $10 \times 3 = $ _____

9. $9 \times 10 = $ _____

10. $10 \times 1 = $ _____

11. $4 \times 10 = $ _____

12. $10 \times 7 = $ _____

13. $10 \times 12 = $ _____

14. $10 \times 15 = $ _____

15. $10 \times 25 = $ _____

16. $10 \times 20 = $ _____

17. $10 \times 32 = $ _____

18. $10 \times 50 = $ _____

When you multiply a non-zero number by 10, it is like writing the number and zero.

19. Look at all the problems above. What is one of the factors in each problem? _____

   What is the ones digit in each product? ____

© School Zone Publishing Company 02215

Multiplying Three Factors

Multiply the way that is easiest for you.

You can find the product of three factors by multiplying them in any order or grouping. This is the **associative property** of multiplication.

Multiply: $2 \times 10 \times 3$

$(2 \times 10) \times 3 =$ $2 \times (10 \times 3) =$ $(2 \times 3) \times 10 =$
$20 \times 3 =$ $2 \times 30 =$ $6 \times 10 =$
60 60 60

Ruffed Lemur

Remember these properties of multiplication:

Commutative Property of Multiplication
If you change the order of the factors, the product is the same.

$3 \times 4 = 12$ and $4 \times 3 = 12$

Identity Property of Multiplication
If you multiply a number and 1, the product is that number.

$1 \times 8 = 8$

Associative Property of Multiplication
If you change the grouping of the factors, the product is the same.

$(2 \times 3) \times 4 = 24$ and $2 \times (3 \times 4) = 24$

Zero Property of Multiplication
If you multiply a number and zero, the product is zero.

$0 \times 7 = 0$

Multiply the factors. Show your work. Be careful!

1. $2 \times 1 \times 8 = \underline{\quad}$

2. $4 \times 10 \times 2 = \underline{\quad}$

3. $5 \times 10 \times 0 = \underline{\quad}$

4. $3 \times 10 \times 3 = \underline{\quad}$

5. $10 \times 10 \times 1 = \underline{\quad}$

6. $2 \times 3 \times 5 = \underline{\quad}$

7. $8 \times 3 \times 2 = \underline{\quad}$

8. $10 \times 2 \times 2 = \underline{\quad}$

9. $3 \times 6 \times 1 = \underline{\quad}$

10. $10 \times 1 \times 10 = \underline{\quad}$

11. $2 \times 10 \times 3 = \underline{\quad}$

12. $9 \times 1 \times 9 = \underline{\quad}$

13. $10 \times 0 \times 10 = \underline{\quad}$

14. $3 \times 3 \times 3 = \underline{\quad}$

15. $9 \times 10 \times 10 = \underline{\quad}$

Remember, multiplication is a shortcut for repeated addition.

1. Add.

$$\begin{array}{r} 11 \\ + 11 \\ \hline 22 \\ + 11 \\ \hline 33 \\ + 11 \\ \hline 44 \\ + 11 \\ \hline \\ + 11 \\ \hline \\ + 11 \\ \hline \\ + 11 \\ \hline \\ + 11 \\ \hline \\ + 11 \\ \hline \\ + 11 \\ \hline \\ + 11 \\ \hline \end{array}$$

2. Multiply.

$11 \times 1 = \underline{\hspace{1cm}}$

$11 \times 2 = \underline{\hspace{1cm}}$

$11 \times 3 = \underline{\hspace{1cm}}$

$11 \times 4 = \underline{\hspace{1cm}}$

$11 \times 5 = \underline{\hspace{1cm}}$

$11 \times 6 = \underline{\hspace{1cm}}$

$11 \times 7 = \underline{\hspace{1cm}}$

$11 \times 8 = \underline{\hspace{1cm}}$

$11 \times 9 = \underline{\hspace{1cm}}$

$11 \times 10 = \underline{\hspace{1cm}}$

$11 \times 11 = \underline{\hspace{1cm}}$

$11 \times 12 = \underline{\hspace{1cm}}$

You can think of 11 as 10 + 1 when you want to remember the 11s.

Tamandua

3. Look at the huge addition problem. Why is it easy to add 11?

_____

4. Look at all the products. What pattern do you see for the first 9 products?

_____

5. What do you think is 11×0? _____ Why?

_____

6. What do you think is 11×13? _____ Why?

_____

          © School Zone Publishing Company 02215

Multiplying by 12

Discus

Looks like there are dozens of problems!

1. Add.

```
    12
  + 12
  ────
    24
  + 12
  ────
    36
  + 12
  ────
    48
  + 12
  ────

  + 12
  ────

  + 12
  ────

  + 12
  ────

  + 12
  ────

  + 12
  ────

  + 12
  ────
```

2. Multiply.

12 x 1 = ____

12 x 2 = ____

12 x 3 = ____

12 x 4 = ____

12 x 5 = ____

12 x 6 = ____

12 x 7 = ____

12 x 8 = ____

12 x 9 = ____

12 x 10 = ____

12 x 11 = ____

12 x 12 = ____

3. Look at the huge addition problem. Is each sum even or odd?

_____

4. Look at all the products. What is the ones digit for each product?

_____

5. What do you think is 12 x 0? ____ Why?

_____

12 objects = 1 dozen
12 inches = 1 foot

6. How many eggs are in 7 dozen?

_____

7. How many inches are in 5 feet?

_____

What I Learned about Multiplication

1. Write an addition and multiplication sentence for the picture.

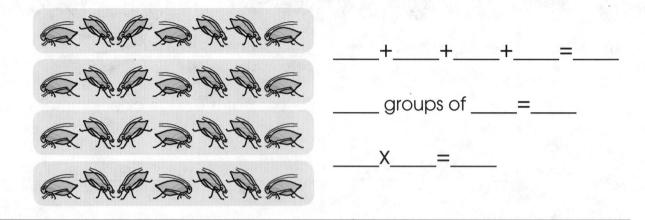

____ + ____ + ____ + ____ = ____

____ groups of ____ = ____

____ X ____ = ____

Draw groups of objects to show each multiplication fact. Then write the answer.

2. $3 \times 8 =$ ____

3. $6 \times 1 =$ ____

4. $7 \times 2 =$ ____

5. $4 \times 4 =$ ____

Long-Horned Grasshopper

Think of multiplication facts and properties to complete each problem.

6. $9 \times 1 =$ ____

7. $6 \times 6 =$ ____

8. $7 \times 3 = 3 \times$ ____

9. $0 \times 8 =$ ____

10. $0 \times 0 =$ ____

11. $4 \times 1 \times 6 =$ ____

Multiply.

12. $7 \times 6 =$ ____

13. $4 \times 9 =$ ____

14. $8 \times 7 =$ ____

15. $8 \times 8 =$ ____

16. $10 \times 7 =$ ____

17. $11 \times 7 =$ ____

18. $12 \times 8 =$ ____

19. $10 \times 10 =$ ____

20. $6 \times 9 =$ ____

© School Zone Publishing Company 02215

Circle the answer.

21. Which of the following does **not** tell about this picture?

A. 4 + 6   **B.** 4 + 4 + 4 + 4 + 4 + 4

C. 6 x 4   **D.** 4 x 6

22. For the 2s multiplication facts, the ones digit is _____ in the products.

A. 1, 2, 3, 4, or 5

B. 2, 4, 6, 8, or 0

C. 1, 2, 4, or 8

D. 0 or 2

23. Which number makes this number sentence true?

$$6 \times 1 = \underline{\quad}$$

A. 0   **B.** 1   **C.** 6   **D.** 60

24. Which number makes this number sentence true?

$$2 \times 4 \times \underline{\quad} = 80$$

A. 6   **B.** 8   **C.** 10   **D.** 12

25. Which number makes this number sentence true?

$$5 \times \underline{\quad} = 0$$

A. 10   **B.** 5   **C.** 1   **D.** 0

26. In the fact 5 x 9 = 45, the 9 is a _____ .

A. addend   **B.** divisor

C. factor   **D.** product

27. How many inches are in 6 feet?

A. 12   **B.** 60

C. 66   **D.** 72

28. How many eggs are in 9 dozen?

A. 12   **B.** 96

C. 108   **D.** 120

29. Which number makes this number sentence true?

$$6 \times \underline{\quad} = 60$$

A. 0   **B.** 1   **C.** 10   **D.** 12

30. 11 + 11 + 11 + 11 + 11 is **not** the same as _____ .

A. 11 x 4   **B.** 5 x 11

C. 44 + 11   **D.** 33 + 11 + 11

Learning about Division

6 divided into 3 groups = 2 in each group

$6 \div 3 = 2$

6 divided into 2 groups = 3 in each group

$6 \div 2 = 3$

Write two division number sentences for the pictures.

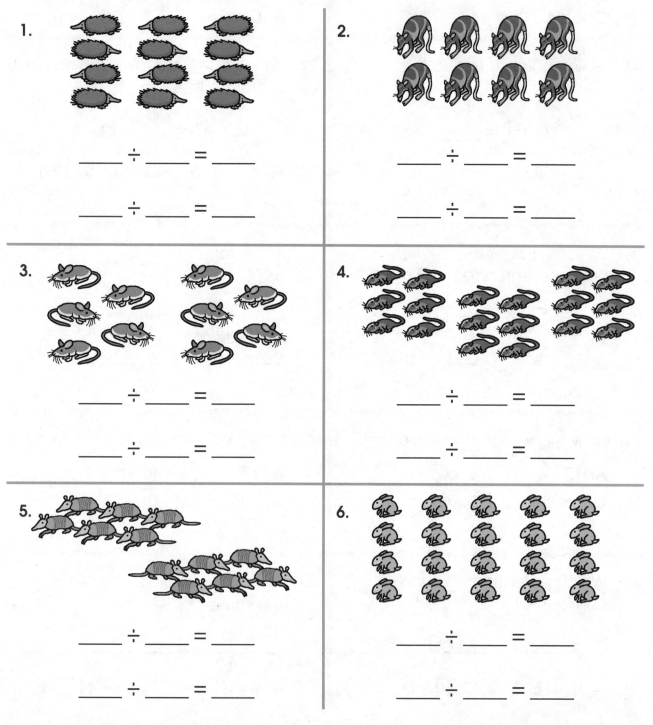

1.

_____ ÷ _____ = _____

_____ ÷ _____ = _____

2.

_____ ÷ _____ = _____

_____ ÷ _____ = _____

3.

_____ ÷ _____ = _____

_____ ÷ _____ = _____

4.

_____ ÷ _____ = _____

_____ ÷ _____ = _____

5.

_____ ÷ _____ = _____

_____ ÷ _____ = _____

6.

_____ ÷ _____ = _____

_____ ÷ _____ = _____

© School Zone Publishing Company 02215

Learning about Division

If you know your multiplication facts, you are ready for division.

Here is a multiplication fact:
$$4 \times 3 = 12$$

Here are two related division facts:
$$12 \div 3 = 4 \text{ and } 12 \div 4 = 3$$

Hawk-Headed Parrot

Write related division facts for each multiplication fact.

1. $8 \times 7 = 56$

   ___ $\div$ ___ $=$ ___

   ___ $\div$ ___ $=$ ___

2. $4 \times 9 = 36$

   ___ $\div$ ___ $=$ ___

   ___ $\div$ ___ $=$ ___

3. $5 \times 5 = 25$

   ___ $\div$ ___ $=$ ___

4. $6 \times 7 = 42$

   ___ $\div$ ___ $=$ ___

   ___ $\div$ ___ $=$ ___

5. $3 \times 8 = 24$

   ___ $\div$ ___ $=$ ___

   ___ $\div$ ___ $=$ ___

6. $2 \times 7 = 14$

   ___ $\div$ ___ $=$ ___

   ___ $\div$ ___ $=$ ___

7. $7 \times 5 = 35$

   ___ $\div$ ___ $=$ ___

   ___ $\div$ ___ $=$ ___

8. $8 \times 9 = 72$

   ___ $\div$ ___ $=$ ___

   ___ $\div$ ___ $=$ ___

9. $4 \times 8 = 32$

   ___ $\div$ ___ $=$ ___

   ___ $\div$ ___ $=$ ___

Solve the problem.

10. Joshua has collected 63 stamps from different countries. He has to divide them into 7 different albums. How many stamps will go into each album?

   _____

Dividing by 2 and 3

There are 15 fish.
There are 3 groups.
There are 5 fish in each group. $15 \div 3 = 5$

Clown Loaches

Draw circles around groups of fish to show the division fact. Then write the answer.

1. $14 \div 2 = \underline{\quad}$

2. $12 \div 3 = \underline{\quad}$

3. $8 \div 2 = \underline{\quad}$

Practice these division facts.
Recall related multiplication facts.

4.
$2 \div 2 = \underline{\quad}$
$4 \div 2 = \underline{\quad}$
$6 \div 2 = \underline{\quad}$
$8 \div 2 = \underline{\quad}$
$10 \div 2 = \underline{\quad}$
$12 \div 2 = \underline{\quad}$
$14 \div 2 = \underline{\quad}$
$16 \div 2 = \underline{\quad}$
$18 \div 2 = \underline{\quad}$

5.
$3 \div 3 = \underline{\quad}$
$6 \div 3 = \underline{\quad}$
$9 \div 3 = \underline{\quad}$
$12 \div 3 = \underline{\quad}$
$15 \div 3 = \underline{\quad}$
$18 \div 3 = \underline{\quad}$
$21 \div 3 = \underline{\quad}$
$24 \div 3 = \underline{\quad}$
$27 \div 3 = \underline{\quad}$

Fill in the blanks.

6. If you know $2 \times 8 = 16$, then you know $16 \div 2 = \underline{\quad}$.

7. If you know $3 \times 7 = 21$, then you know $21 \div \underline{\quad} = \underline{\quad}$.

8. If you know $2 \times 9 = \underline{\quad}$, then you know $\underline{\quad} \div 2 = \underline{\quad}$.

9. If you know $\underline{\quad} \times 3 = 3$, then you know $\underline{\quad} \div \underline{\quad} = \underline{\quad}$.

---

10. Look at the facts above. What is a number divided by itself? $\underline{\quad}$

   © School Zone Publishing Company 02215

Dividing by 4 and 5

Circle the fish to show the division fact. Write the answer.

1. $20 \div 4 =$ _____

2. $30 \div 5 =$ _____

Practice these division facts.
Recall related multiplication facts.

3. $4 \div 4 =$ _____
$8 \div 4 =$ _____
$12 \div 4 =$ _____
$16 \div 4 =$ _____
$20 \div 4 =$ _____
$24 \div 4 =$ _____
$28 \div 4 =$ _____
$32 \div 4 =$ _____
$36 \div 4 =$ _____

4. $5 \div 5 =$ _____
$10 \div 5 =$ _____
$15 \div 5 =$ _____
$20 \div 5 =$ _____
$25 \div 5 =$ _____
$30 \div 5 =$ _____
$35 \div 5 =$ _____
$40 \div 5 =$ _____
$45 \div 5 =$ _____

Divide.

5. $12 \div 4 =$ _____
$10 \div 5 =$ _____
$32 \div 4 =$ _____
$40 \div 5 =$ _____
$4 \div 4 =$ _____
$20 \div 5 =$ _____
$36 \div 4 =$ _____
$28 \div 4 =$ _____
$5 \div 5 =$ _____
$24 \div 4 =$ _____

Surubim

Giant Armadillo

Practice these division facts.
Recall related multiplication facts.

1. $6 \div 6 =$ _____
   $12 \div 6 =$ _____
   $18 \div 6 =$ _____
   $24 \div 6 =$ _____
   $30 \div 6 =$ _____
   $36 \div 6 =$ _____
   $42 \div 6 =$ _____
   $48 \div 6 =$ _____
   $54 \div 6 =$ _____

2. $7 \div 7 =$ _____
   $14 \div 7 =$ _____
   $21 \div 7 =$ _____
   $28 \div 7 =$ _____
   $35 \div 7 =$ _____
   $42 \div 7 =$ _____
   $49 \div 7 =$ _____
   $56 \div 7 =$ _____
   $63 \div 7 =$ _____

3. Find the missing numbers.

   $36 \div$ _____ $= 6$

   _____ $\div 7 = 3$

   $48 \div 6 =$ _____

   _____ $\div 7 = 7$

   $18 \div$ _____ $= 3$

   $63 \div$ _____ $= 9$

   $21 \div$ _____ $= 7$

   _____ $\div 7 = 8$

   _____ $\div 6 = 9$

© School Zone Publishing Company 02215

Dividing by 8 and 9

Banded Linsang

Practice these division facts.
Recall related multiplication facts.

1. $8 \div 8 = \underline{\hspace{1cm}}$
   $16 \div 8 = \underline{\hspace{1cm}}$
   $24 \div 8 = \underline{\hspace{1cm}}$
   $32 \div 8 = \underline{\hspace{1cm}}$
   $40 \div 8 = \underline{\hspace{1cm}}$
   $48 \div 8 = \underline{\hspace{1cm}}$
   $56 \div 8 = \underline{\hspace{1cm}}$
   $64 \div 8 = \underline{\hspace{1cm}}$
   $72 \div 8 = \underline{\hspace{1cm}}$

2. $9 \div 9 = \underline{\hspace{1cm}}$
   $18 \div 9 = \underline{\hspace{1cm}}$
   $27 \div 9 = \underline{\hspace{1cm}}$
   $36 \div 9 = \underline{\hspace{1cm}}$
   $45 \div 9 = \underline{\hspace{1cm}}$
   $54 \div 9 = \underline{\hspace{1cm}}$
   $63 \div 9 = \underline{\hspace{1cm}}$
   $72 \div 9 = \underline{\hspace{1cm}}$
   $81 \div 9 = \underline{\hspace{1cm}}$

Write a fact family for each group of numbers.

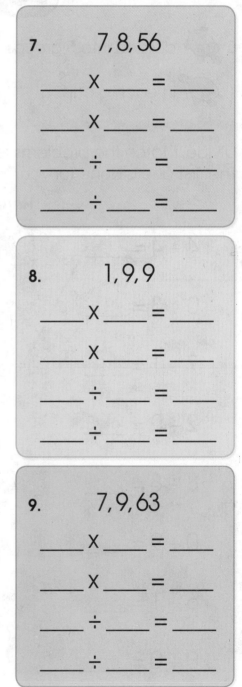

7.　　　7, 8, 56

$\underline{\hspace{1cm}} \times \underline{\hspace{1cm}} = \underline{\hspace{1cm}}$

$\underline{\hspace{1cm}} \times \underline{\hspace{1cm}} = \underline{\hspace{1cm}}$

$\underline{\hspace{1cm}} \div \underline{\hspace{1cm}} = \underline{\hspace{1cm}}$

$\underline{\hspace{1cm}} \div \underline{\hspace{1cm}} = \underline{\hspace{1cm}}$

8.　　　1, 9, 9

$\underline{\hspace{1cm}} \times \underline{\hspace{1cm}} = \underline{\hspace{1cm}}$

$\underline{\hspace{1cm}} \times \underline{\hspace{1cm}} = \underline{\hspace{1cm}}$

$\underline{\hspace{1cm}} \div \underline{\hspace{1cm}} = \underline{\hspace{1cm}}$

$\underline{\hspace{1cm}} \div \underline{\hspace{1cm}} = \underline{\hspace{1cm}}$

9.　　　7, 9, 63

$\underline{\hspace{1cm}} \times \underline{\hspace{1cm}} = \underline{\hspace{1cm}}$

$\underline{\hspace{1cm}} \times \underline{\hspace{1cm}} = \underline{\hspace{1cm}}$

$\underline{\hspace{1cm}} \div \underline{\hspace{1cm}} = \underline{\hspace{1cm}}$

$\underline{\hspace{1cm}} \div \underline{\hspace{1cm}} = \underline{\hspace{1cm}}$

Fill in the missing numbers for each fact family.

3. $5 \times 8 = \underline{\hspace{1cm}}$　　　$8 \times \underline{\hspace{1cm}} = 40$
   $40 \div 5 = \underline{\hspace{1cm}}$　　　$40 \div 8 = \underline{\hspace{1cm}}$

4. $9 \times \underline{\hspace{1cm}} = 54$　　　$6 \times 9 = \underline{\hspace{1cm}}$
   $54 \div 9 = \underline{\hspace{1cm}}$　　　$\underline{\hspace{1cm}} \div 6 = 9$

5. $\underline{\hspace{1cm}} \times 8 = 72$　　　$8 \times \underline{\hspace{1cm}} = 72$
   $72 \div 8 = \underline{\hspace{1cm}}$　　　$72 \div \underline{\hspace{1cm}} = 8$

6. $8 \times 8 = \underline{\hspace{1cm}}$　　　$64 \div \underline{\hspace{1cm}} = 8$

Dividing with 1 and 0

$5 \div 5 = 1$

$5 \div 1 = 5$

Yellow-Spotted
River Turtle

5 🐢 divided into 5 groups

1 🐢 in each group

5 🐢 divided into 1 group

5 🐢 in the group

Divide. Match the problems to the division rules.
The first one is done for you.

Here are some division rules:

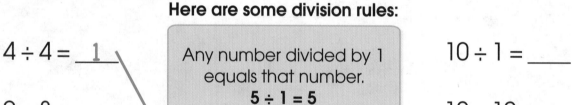

$4 \div 4 = \underline{1}$

$0 \div 3 = \underline{}$

$7 \div 1 = \underline{}$

$2 \div 0 = \underline{}$

$8 \div 8 = \underline{}$

$0 \div 9 = \underline{}$

$6 \div 1 = \underline{}$

$0 \div 0 = \underline{}$

Any number divided by 1
equals that number.
$5 \div 1 = 5$

Any non-zero number
divided by itself is 1.
$5 \div 5 = 1$

Zero divided by any non-
zero number equals 0.
$0 \div 5 = 0$

You cannot divide by zero.
You **cannot** do **$5 \div 0$**.

$10 \div 1 = \underline{}$

$12 \div 12 = \underline{}$

$0 \div 11 = \underline{}$

$25 \div 25 = \underline{}$

$15 \div 0 = \underline{}$

$0 \div 25 = \underline{}$

$12 \div 1 = \underline{}$

$11 \div 11 = \underline{}$

© School Zone Publishing Company 02215

Writing Division Facts Two Ways

You can write a division problem two ways.
There are three parts to a division problem.

$12 \div 3 = 4$

Dividend
Divisor
Quotient

$3\overline{)12}$ ← Quotient
← Dividend

Divisor

Golden Lion
Tamarin

Rewrite each division problem.

1. $36 \div 9 = 4$ $\overline{)}$

2. $10 \div 2 = 5$ $\overline{)}$

3. $56 \div 8 = 7$ $\overline{)}$

4. $63 \div 7 = 9$ $\overline{)}$

Complete each problem by finding the divisor and quotient.
Hint: there may be more than one answer for each problem.

5. $18 \div \underline{} = \underline{}$

6. $\underline{}\overline{)30}$

7. $\underline{}\overline{)45}$

8. $54 \div \underline{} = \underline{}$

9. $72 \div \underline{} = \underline{}$

10. $\underline{}\overline{)7}$

Divide.

11. $36 \div 4 = \underline{}$

12. $6\overline{)42}$

13. $27 \div 3 = \underline{}$

14. $7\overline{)63}$

15. $56 \div 8 = \underline{}$

16. $9\overline{)81}$

17. $8\overline{)8}$

18. $40 \div 5 = \underline{}$

19. $6\overline{)0}$

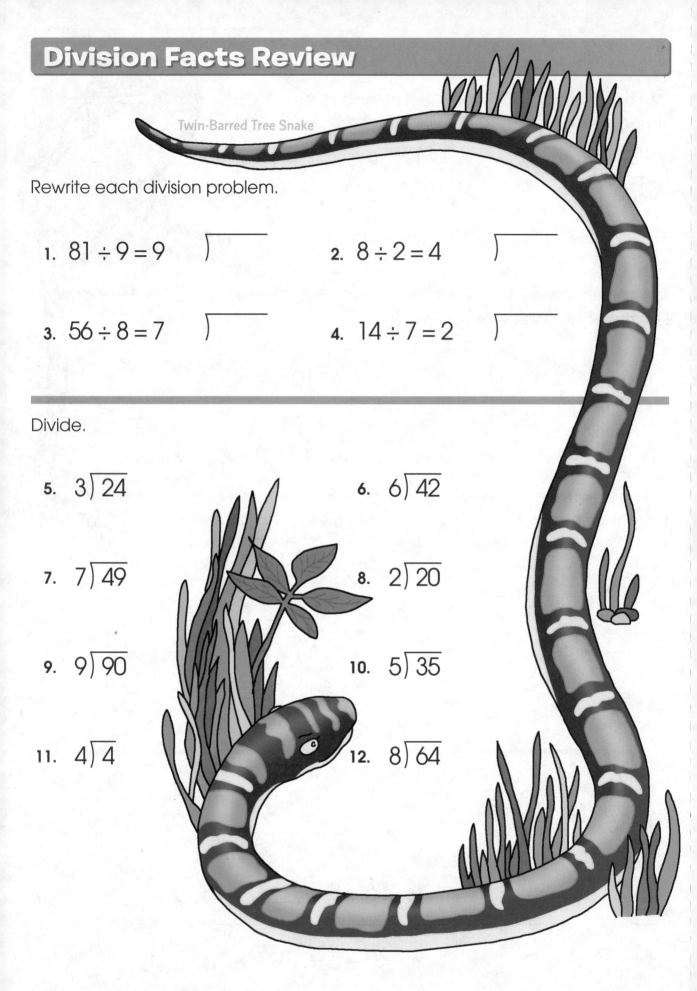

Twin-Barred Tree Snake

Rewrite each division problem.

1. $81 \div 9 = 9$

2. $8 \div 2 = 4$

3. $56 \div 8 = 7$

4. $14 \div 7 = 2$

Divide.

5. $3\overline{)24}$

6. $6\overline{)42}$

7. $7\overline{)49}$

8. $2\overline{)20}$

9. $9\overline{)90}$

10. $5\overline{)35}$

11. $4\overline{)4}$

12. $8\overline{)64}$

© School Zone Publishing Company　02215

Multiplication and Division Word Problems

To solve division problems, look for clue words like **how many groups** or **how many in each group**.

Write and solve a number sentence. Label the answer.

Joshua has 20 fish. He divided them equally into 4 fish bowls. How many fish are in each bowl?

$$\underline{20} \div \underline{4} = \underline{5}$$
$$\underline{5} \qquad \underline{fish}$$

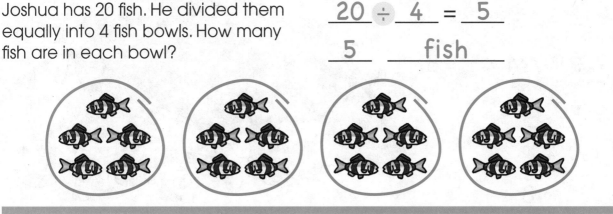

Write and solve a number sentence for each problem. Label your answer.

1. Joshua has 24 Brazil nuts that he has to divide among 6 friends. How many nuts will each friend get?

   ____ ⦿ ____ = ____

   ____ _____

2. Joshua and his two friends each bought 8 bananas. How many bananas did all 3 of them buy?

   ____ ⦿ ____ = ____

   ____ _____

3. Joshua put 6 stickers in each row on an album page. If there are 7 rows on each page, what is the total number of stickers on each page?

   ____ ⦿ ____ = ____

   ____ _____

4. Joshua has 9 toy boats. He put an equal number of them into 3 different boxes. How many boats are in each box?

   ____ ⦿ ____ = ____

   ____ _____

Combining Multiplication and Division

Here's a fun activity for you using both multiplication and division. Multiply and/or divide the first four numbers in order to make the fifth number. You may want to use a calculator.

$9 \bigcirc 9 \bigcirc 4 \bigcirc 2 = 8$

$9 \div 9 \times 4 \times 2 = 8$

1×4

4×2

8

Brazilian Tapirs

Your turn!

1. $6 \bigcirc 5 \bigcirc 3 \bigcirc 2 = 5$

2. $10 \bigcirc 5 \bigcirc 4 \bigcirc 2 = 4$

3. $49 \bigcirc 7 \bigcirc 6 \bigcirc 6 = 7$

4. $81 \bigcirc 9 \bigcirc 3 \bigcirc 6 = 18$

5. $2 \bigcirc 2 \bigcirc 2 \bigcirc 2 = 1$

6. $64 \bigcirc 8 \bigcirc 8 \bigcirc 1 = 1$

7. $8 \bigcirc 5 \bigcirc 4 \bigcirc 3 = 30$

8. $24 \bigcirc 8 \bigcirc 9 \bigcirc 3 = 9$

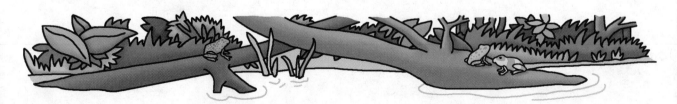

© School Zone Publishing Company 02215

Complete the problems.
Then write the numbers in the puzzle.

Across

1. 5 groups of 8 is _____.

2. $7 \times 8 =$ _____

3. $27 \div 9 =$ _____

4. $8 \times$ _____ $= 64$

5. _____ $\div 6 = 4$

6. 9 groups of 4 is _____.

7. $2 \times 7 =$ _____

8. $5 \times 4 =$ _____

9. $9 \times 8 =$ _____

10. $6 \div$ _____ $= 6$

11. _____ $\times 5 = 30$

12. $4 \times 7 =$ _____

13. _____ $\div 4 = 6$

14. $8 \times 5 =$ _____

15. _____ $\div 7 = 4$

Down

1. $8 \times 6 =$ _____

2. _____ $\div 6 = 9$

3. $6 \times 6 =$ _____

5. _____ $\div 8 = 3$

6. 5 groups of 6 is _____.

7. _____ $\div 3 = 4$

9. _____ $\div 8 = 9$

10. 3 groups of 6 is _____.

11. _____ $\div 8 = 8$

12. $5 \times 4 =$ _____

13. $4 \times 7 =$ _____

Jaguarundi

© School Zone Publishing Company 02215 Reviewing Multiplication and Division Facts (3.OA.1,4,7)

What I Learned about Division

1. Write a multiplication and division sentence for the picture.

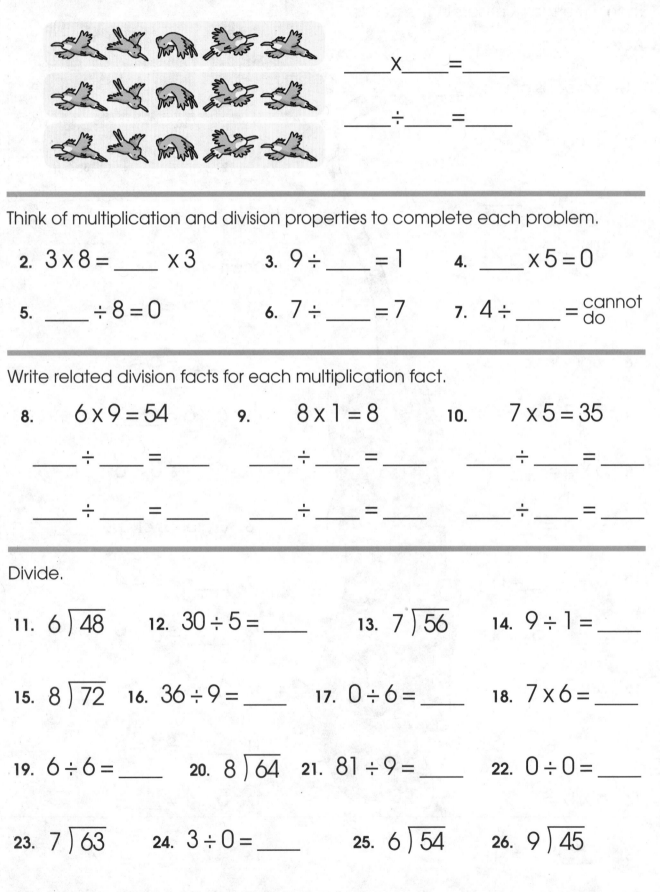

____ X ____ = ____

____ ÷ ____ = ____

Think of multiplication and division properties to complete each problem.

2. $3 \times 8 =$ ____ $\times 3$ 3. $9 \div$ ____ $= 1$ 4. ____ $\times 5 = 0$

5. ____ $\div 8 = 0$ 6. $7 \div$ ____ $= 7$ 7. $4 \div$ ____ $= \begin{smallmatrix}\text{cannot}\\\text{do}\end{smallmatrix}$

Write related division facts for each multiplication fact.

8. $6 \times 9 = 54$ 9. $8 \times 1 = 8$ 10. $7 \times 5 = 35$

____ ÷ ____ = ____   ____ ÷ ____ = ____   ____ ÷ ____ = ____

____ ÷ ____ = ____   ____ ÷ ____ = ____   ____ ÷ ____ = ____

Divide.

11. $6\overline{)48}$ 12. $30 \div 5 =$ ____   13. $7\overline{)56}$ 14. $9 \div 1 =$ ____

15. $8\overline{)72}$ 16. $36 \div 9 =$ ____   17. $0 \div 6 =$ ____   18. $7 \times 6 =$ ____

19. $6 \div 6 =$ ____   20. $8\overline{)64}$ 21. $81 \div 9 =$ ____   22. $0 \div 0 =$ ____

23. $7\overline{)63}$ 24. $3 \div 0 =$ ____   25. $6\overline{)54}$ 26. $9\overline{)45}$

© School Zone Publishing Company 02215

Circle the answer.

27. Which number sentence does **not** tell about this picture?

   A. $12 \div 6 = 2$ **B.** $12 - 6 = 2$

   C. $12 \div 2 = 6$ **D.** $6 \times 2 = 12$

28. Joshua put 36 shells into 4 equal groups. Which number sentence would you use to find how many shells are in each group?

   A. $4 \times 36 = \underline{}$

   B. $4 + 36 = \underline{}$

   C. $36 \div 4 = \underline{}$

   D. $36 - 4 = \underline{}$

29. Which fact does **not** belong in the same fact family with the other choices?

   A. $5 \times 6 = 30$ **B.** $30 \div 5 = 6$

   C. $30 \times 5 = 6$ **D.** $30 \div 6 = 5$

30. Which option makes this number sentence true?

$$8 \div 0 = \underline{}$$

   A. 0   **B.** 8   **C.** 80   **D.** cannot do

31. Which word names the part of this problem pointed to by the arrow?

$$6 \overline{)24} \leftarrow \overset{4}{}$$

   A. quotient   **B.** product

   C. divisor   **D.** dividend

32. Which number makes this number sentence true?

$$9 \div 3 = \underline{}$$

   A. 0   **B.** 1   **C.** 3   **D.** 27

33. Which number makes this number sentence true?

$$7 \div \underline{} = 7$$

   A. 0   **B.** 1   **C.** 7   **D.** 49

34. Which of the following number sentences cannot be done?

   A. $0 \div 4$ **B.** $4 \div 4$

   C. $4 \div 1$ **D.** $4 \div 0$

Multiplication Patterns

White-Lipped Peccary

If you know your multiplication facts, you can find these products mentally. Look for a pattern.

$3 \times 4 = 12$ 3×4 ones $= 12$ ones

$3 \times 40 = 120$ 3×4 tens $= 12$ tens

$3 \times 400 = 1,200$ 3×4 hundreds $= 12$ hundreds

Practice the facts.

1. $8 \times 1 =$ _____

   $8 \times 10 =$ _____

   $8 \times 100 =$ _____

2. $7 \times 9 =$ _____

   $7 \times 90 =$ _____

   $7 \times 900 =$ _____

Fill in the blanks.

3. 6×1 ten $=$ __6__ tens $=$ __60__

4. 4×4 hundreds $=$ _____ hundreds $=$ _____

5. 3×9 hundreds $=$ _____ hundreds $=$ _____

6. 8×7 tens $=$ _____ tens $=$ _____

7. 5×8 tens $=$ _____ tens $=$ _____

8. 6×9 hundreds $=$ _____ hundreds $=$ _____

Multiply mentally.

9. $7 \times 100 =$ _____

10. $4 \times 90 =$ _____

11. $3 \times 500 =$ _____

12. $40 \times 7 =$ _____

13. $300 \times 8 =$ _____

14. $9 \times 50 =$ _____

15. $600 \times 7 =$ _____

16. $8 \times 50 =$ _____

17. $8 \times 900 =$ _____

---

18. Complete the chart.

X	10	30	80	100	400	900
5						
7				700		
8			640			

© School Zone Publishing Company 02215

Estimating Products

Use rounding to estimate products.

Joshua has 3 tanks of fish.
There are 37 fish in each tank.
About how many fish is this?

> If the number is 5 or more, round up.
> If the number is 4 or less, round down.

3×37
↓   ↓
$3 \times 40 = 120$ Round 37 to 40.   There are about 120 fish.

```
40
39
38
37 ↑
36
35
34
33
32 ↓
31
30
```

Estimate the product by rounding.

1. 4×62
   ___ X ___ = ___

2. 6×75
   ___ X ___ = ___

3. 3×191
   ___ X ___ = ___

4. 637×8
   ___ X ___ = ___

5. 7×213
   ___ X ___ = ___

6. 5×807
   ___ X ___ = ___

Estimate the product.

7. 3×71 _____

8. 4×795 _____

9. 7×678 _____

10. 459×4 _____

11. 2×925 _____

12. 88×6 _____

13. 5×304 _____

14. 7×77 _____

15. 605×9 _____

Solve the problem.

16. Joshua has 3 photo albums. There are 68 photographs in each album. About how many photographs are in the albums? _____

17. Joshua rides the bus to school. There are 42 students on each bus. About how many students are on 6 buses? _____

Multiplying Two-Digit Numbers

If you know the multiplication facts, you can multiply any two numbers together.

Multiply the ones.

```
    tens ones
      2  3
  x      3
  ─────────
         9
```

Multiply the tens.

```
    tens ones
      2  3
  x      3
  ─────────
      6  9
```

Quetzal

Multiply.

1. 14
    x 2
    ────

2. 12
    x 4
    ────

3. 23
    x 2
    ────

4. 33
    x 3
    ────

5. 24
    x 2
    ────

6. 11
    x 7
    ────

7. 32
    x 3
    ────

8. 10
    x 4
    ────

9. 13
    x 2
    ────

Solve the problem.

10. Joshua is filling 3 pages in his journal per day. How many pages will he fill in 12 days?

_____

© School Zone Publishing Company 02215

Multiplying with Regrouping

Sometimes you need to regroup when you multiply.

Multiply the ones.
Regroup.

$$
\begin{array}{r}
\overset{3}{4}5 \\
\times\ 7 \\
\hline
5
\end{array}
$$

7 ones x 5 ones = 35 ones
Regroup as 3 tens and 5
ones.

Multiply the tens.
Add regrouped ones.

$$
\begin{array}{r}
\overset{3}{4}5 \\
\times\ 7 \\
\hline
315
\end{array}
$$

7 ones x 4 tens = 28 tens
28 tens + 3 tens = 31 tens
31 tens is 3 hundreds
and 1 ten.

Paca

Multiply.

1. $\begin{array}{r} 42 \\ \times\ 6 \\ \hline \end{array}$
2. $\begin{array}{r} 98 \\ \times\ 2 \\ \hline \end{array}$
3. $\begin{array}{r} 74 \\ \times\ 4 \\ \hline \end{array}$
4. $\begin{array}{r} 34 \\ \times\ 3 \\ \hline \end{array}$
5. $\begin{array}{r} 78 \\ \times\ 2 \\ \hline \end{array}$
6. $\begin{array}{r} 64 \\ \times\ 5 \\ \hline \end{array}$

7. $\begin{array}{r} 63 \\ \times\ 9 \\ \hline \end{array}$
8. $\begin{array}{r} 18 \\ \times\ 3 \\ \hline \end{array}$
9. $\begin{array}{r} 55 \\ \times\ 5 \\ \hline \end{array}$
10. $\begin{array}{r} 19 \\ \times\ 9 \\ \hline \end{array}$
11. $\begin{array}{r} 28 \\ \times\ 3 \\ \hline \end{array}$
12. $\begin{array}{r} 45 \\ \times\ 5 \\ \hline \end{array}$

Try these!

13. $4 \times 2 \times 3 =$ _____

14. $5 \times 2 \times 8 =$ _____

15. $6 \times 2 \times 3 =$ _____

© School Zone Publishing Company 02215

Multiplying Three-Digit Numbers

Multiply the ones.
Regroup.

```
    1
  452
x   6
─────
    2
```

6 ones x 2 ones = 12 ones
Regroup as 1 ten and 2 ones.

Multiply the tens.
Add regrouped ones.
Regroup.

```
  3 1
  452
x   6
─────
   12
```

6 ones x 5 tens = 30 tens
30 tens + 1 ten = 31 tens
Regroup as 3 hundreds
and 1 ten.

Multiply the hundreds.
Add regrouped tens.

```
  3 1
  452
x   6
─────
2,712
```

6 ones x 4 hundreds = 24 hundreds
24 hundreds + 3 hundreds = 27 hundreds

Estimate the product: 6 x 452 is about 6 x 500 = 3,000

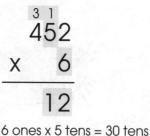

Multiply. Estimate to check your answer.

Electric Eel

1.
```
  126     Estimate
x   4   x
```

2.
```
  472     Estimate
x   2   x
```

3.
```
  975     Estimate
x   4   x
```

4.
```
  134     Estimate
x   7   x
```

5.
```
  813     Estimate
x   3   x
```

6.
```
  144     Estimate
x   8   x
```

7.
```
  135     Estimate
x   2   x
```

8.
```
  292     Estimate
x   5   x
```

9.
```
  224     Estimate
x   9   x
```

© School Zone Publishing Company 02215

More Multiplication

Multiply. Estimate to check your answer.

Paradise Tanager

1.
```
    78     Estimate
x    4   x _____
_____
```

2.
```
    56     Estimate
x    8   x _____
_____
```

3.
```
    26     Estimate
x    9   x _____
_____
```

4.
```
   213     Estimate
x    4   x _____
_____
```

5.
```
   183     Estimate
x    7   x _____
_____
```

6.
```
   491     Estimate
x    6   x _____
_____
```

7.
```
   169     Estimate
x    3   x _____
_____
```

8.
```
   555     Estimate
x    4   x _____
_____
```

9.
```
   732     Estimate
x    5   x _____
_____
```

Solve the problem.

10. The largest bird is the ostrich. An ostrich can weigh up to 345 pounds. How much would 4 ostriches weigh?

_____

11. How many ostriches might weigh about one ton? A ton is 2,000 pounds.

_____

Jaguar

Multiplying with Zeros

Estimate to check.
8 x 300 = 2,400

$$\begin{array}{r} {}^{5} \\ 307 \\ \times 8 \\ \hline 2,456 \end{array}$$

Multiply the ones. Regroup.
Multiply the tens.
8 x 0 = 0 and 0 + 5 = 5
Multiply the hundreds.

Philippine Flying
Lemurs

Multiply. Estimate to check your answer.

1.
$$\begin{array}{r} 301 \\ \times 3 \\ \hline \end{array}$$

2.
$$\begin{array}{r} 190 \\ \times 3 \\ \hline \end{array}$$

3.
$$\begin{array}{r} 390 \\ \times 5 \\ \hline \end{array}$$

4.
$$\begin{array}{r} 705 \\ \times 6 \\ \hline \end{array}$$

5.
$$\begin{array}{r} 402 \\ \times 6 \\ \hline \end{array}$$

6.
$$\begin{array}{r} 450 \\ \times 5 \\ \hline \end{array}$$

7.
$$\begin{array}{r} 306 \\ \times 5 \\ \hline \end{array}$$

8.
$$\begin{array}{r} 409 \\ \times 2 \\ \hline \end{array}$$

9.
$$\begin{array}{r} 204 \\ \times 7 \\ \hline \end{array}$$

10.
$$\begin{array}{r} 350 \\ \times 9 \\ \hline \end{array}$$

11.
$$\begin{array}{r} 406 \\ \times 9 \\ \hline \end{array}$$

12.
$$\begin{array}{r} 670 \\ \times 8 \\ \hline \end{array}$$

Find the missing digits.

13.
$$\begin{array}{r} 3\,\bigcirc\,2 \\ \times 8 \\ \hline 2,\bigcirc16 \end{array}$$

14.
$$\begin{array}{r} 605 \\ \times \bigcirc \\ \hline 4,\bigcirc40 \end{array}$$

15.
$$\begin{array}{r} 34\,\bigcirc \\ \times 5 \\ \hline 1,\bigcirc00 \end{array}$$

16.
$$\begin{array}{r} 2\,\bigcirc\,0 \\ \times 7 \\ \hline 1,8\,\bigcirc\,0 \end{array}$$

© School Zone Publishing Company 02215

Multiplying Four-Digit Numbers

$$\overset{2\quad 1\ 1}{5,432}$$
$$\times \qquad 6$$
$$\overline{32,592}$$

Multiply the ones. Regroup.
Multiply the tens. Regroup.
Multiply the hundreds. Regroup.
Multiply the thousands. 6 x 5 = 30 + 2 = 32

Multiply.

1. 2,222
    x   3

2. 3,141
    x   5

3. 1,338
    x   6

4. 9,214
    x   4

5. 7,768
    x   2

6. 5,261
    x   3

7. 3,105
    x   7

8. 2,025
    x   8

9. 6,350
    x   5

Solve the problem.

10. The largest reptile is the saltwater crocodile. A
    saltwater crocodile weighs about 1,500 pounds.
    How much would a half dozen of them weigh?

Saltwater Crocodile

Multiplying Money

When you write amounts of money as dollars and cents, there are always two places for cents. Remember to put a decimal point in the answer after you multiply.

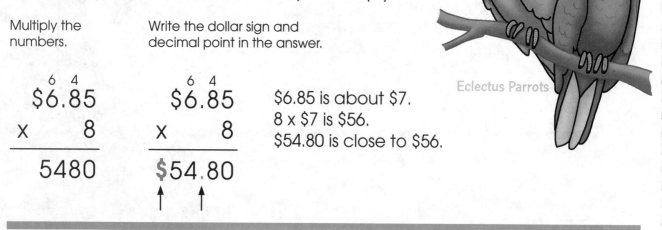

Multiply the numbers.

```
  6 4
$6.85
x    8
─────
 5480
```

Write the dollar sign and decimal point in the answer.

```
  6 4
$6.85
x    8
─────
$54.80
  ↑  ↑
```

$6.85 is about $7.
8 x $7 is $56.
$54.80 is close to $56.

Eclectus Parrots

Estimate the product. Round each amount to the nearest dollar or 10 dollars. The first one is done for you.

1. $2.93
    x   6
    ─────
    $3x6=$18

2. $8.06
    x   7
    ─────

3. $42.50
    x   3
    ─────

4. $0.89
    x   9
    ─────

Multiply.

5. $2.93
    x   6
    ─────

6. $8.06
    x   7
    ─────

7. $42.50
    x   3
    ─────

8. $0.89
    x   9
    ─────

9. $4.75
    x   6
    ─────

10. $7.49
    x   4
    ─────

11. $38.29
    x   3
    ─────

12. $0.98
    x   6
    ─────

© School Zone Publishing Company 02215

Multiplication Word Problems

Look at the prices above to solve each problem.
Read the problems very carefully!

1. Joshua bought 3 t-shirts.
    How much did the t-shirts cost?

    _____

2. Joshua also bought 6 pairs of socks.
    How much did the socks cost?

    _____

3. Joshua and 3 friends each bought a
    new backpack. How much did all the
    backpacks cost?

    _____

4. The 4 campers bought 5 different bird
    books. How much did they spend on
    the books?

    _____

5. The 4 campers bought 2 boxes of raisins
    each for a snack on their hike. How much
    did they pay for all the boxes of raisins?

    _____

6. The 4 campers each bought a pair of
    sunglasses and a bottle of sunscreen. What
    was the total cost of these items for all the
    campers?

    _____

Here's a shortcut for multiplying with multiples of 10. Multiply the non-zero numbers. Then count all the zeros and write that many zeros in the product.

$$\begin{array}{r} 80 \\ \times\ 40 \\ \hline 3,200 \end{array}$$

8 x 4 = 32
There are two zeros.
The product is 32 followed by two zeros.

Manatees

Multiply.

1. $\begin{array}{r} 20 \\ \times\ 30 \\ \hline \end{array}$

2. $\begin{array}{r} 80 \\ \times\ 70 \\ \hline \end{array}$

3. $\begin{array}{r} 60 \\ \times\ 50 \\ \hline \end{array}$

4. $\begin{array}{r} 20 \\ \times\ 80 \\ \hline \end{array}$

5. $\begin{array}{r} 60 \\ \times\ 60 \\ \hline \end{array}$

6. $\begin{array}{r} 70 \\ \times\ 60 \\ \hline \end{array}$

7. $\begin{array}{r} 50 \\ \times\ 80 \\ \hline \end{array}$

8. $\begin{array}{r} 90 \\ \times\ 40 \\ \hline \end{array}$

9. $\begin{array}{r} 30 \\ \times\ 40 \\ \hline \end{array}$

10. $\begin{array}{r} 90 \\ \times\ 30 \\ \hline \end{array}$

---

11. Complete the chart.

X	10	20	40	50	60	80
10						
30						
60						
70						
90						

Knowing how to multiply with multiples of 10 will help you estimate products on the next few pages.

© School Zone Publishing Company 02215

Multiplying by Two-Digit Numbers

Multiply by ones to find a partial product.

$$\begin{array}{r} \overset{3}{54} \\ \times\ 38 \\ \hline 432 \end{array}$$

$8 \times 54 = 432$

Multiply by tens to find another partial product.

$$\begin{array}{r} \overset{1}{54} \\ \times\ 38 \\ \hline 432 \\ 1620 \end{array}$$

3 tens x 54 = 162 tens
162 tens is 1,620.

Add the partial products.

$$\begin{array}{r} 54 \\ \times\ 38 \\ \hline 432 \\ +1620 \\ \hline 2,052 \end{array}$$

432 + 1620 = 2,052

Victoria Crowned Pigeon

Multiply. Estimate to check your answer.

1.
$$\begin{array}{r} 31 \\ \times\ 77 \\ \hline \end{array}$$
Estimate
x _____

2.
$$\begin{array}{r} 46 \\ \times\ 22 \\ \hline \end{array}$$
Estimate
x _____

3.
$$\begin{array}{r} 93 \\ \times\ 11 \\ \hline \end{array}$$
Estimate
x _____

4.
$$\begin{array}{r} 84 \\ \times\ 17 \\ \hline \end{array}$$
Estimate
x _____

5.
$$\begin{array}{r} 53 \\ \times\ 44 \\ \hline \end{array}$$
Estimate
x _____

6.
$$\begin{array}{r} 62 \\ \times\ 25 \\ \hline \end{array}$$
Estimate
x _____

Solve the problem.

7. Joshua has 23 classmates. He promised to send each of them a postcard from all of the 12 cities he plans to visit. How many postcards will he send? _____

Multiplying Two–Digit Numbers (4.NBT.5)

Multiplying by Multiples of Ten

Multiply by ones.
Multiply by tens.
Add partial products.

Use a shortcut.
Write a zero in the ones place.
Multiply by tens.

$$
\begin{array}{r}
1 \\
54 \\
\times\ 30 \\
\hline
00 \quad \leftarrow 0 \times 54 \\
+1620 \quad \leftarrow 30 \times 54 \\
\hline
1{,}620
\end{array}
$$

$$
\begin{array}{r}
1 \\
54 \\
\times\ 30 \\
\hline
1{,}620
\end{array}
$$

Multiply.

1. $\begin{array}{r} 32 \\ \times\ 30 \\ \hline \end{array}$
2. $\begin{array}{r} 78 \\ \times\ 20 \\ \hline \end{array}$
3. $\begin{array}{r} 63 \\ \times\ 50 \\ \hline \end{array}$
4. $\begin{array}{r} 29 \\ \times\ 70 \\ \hline \end{array}$

5. $\begin{array}{r} 31 \\ \times\ 20 \\ \hline \end{array}$
6. $\begin{array}{r} 43 \\ \times\ 60 \\ \hline \end{array}$
7. $\begin{array}{r} 25 \\ \times\ 40 \\ \hline \end{array}$
8. $\begin{array}{r} 84 \\ \times\ 40 \\ \hline \end{array}$

9. $\begin{array}{r} 23 \\ \times\ 30 \\ \hline \end{array}$
10. $\begin{array}{r} 56 \\ \times\ 60 \\ \hline \end{array}$
11. $\begin{array}{r} 71 \\ \times\ 50 \\ \hline \end{array}$
12. $\begin{array}{r} 99 \\ \times\ 40 \\ \hline \end{array}$

Orchids

Solve the problem.

13. About 45 species of orchids were found blooming in a single rainforest tree. If 20 trees had the same number of different species, how many kinds of orchids would you find? _____

© School Zone Publishing Company 02215

Greatest and Least Products

Use a digit only once in each problem to find the product. You may use a calculator.

1. Find the greatest product.

X ⬤ ⬤
_____

2. Find the least product.

X ⬤ ⬤
_____

3. Find the greatest product.

X ⬤ ⬤ ⬤
_____

4. Find the least product.

X ⬤ ⬤ ⬤
_____

5. Find the greatest product.

X ⬤,⬤ ⬤ ⬤
_____

6. Find the least product.

X ⬤,⬤ ⬤ ⬤
_____

7. Find the greatest product.

X ⬤ ⬤ ⬤
_____

8. Find the least product.

X ⬤ ⬤ ⬤
_____

Tokay Gecko

© School Zone Publishing Company 02215

Multiply mentally.

1. $6 \times 10 = \underline{\hspace{2cm}}$ 2. $7 \times 50 = \underline{\hspace{2cm}}$ 3. $400 \times 2 = \underline{\hspace{2cm}}$

4. $8 \times 700 = \underline{\hspace{2cm}}$ 5. $30 \times 30 = \underline{\hspace{2cm}}$ 6. $60 \times 90 = \underline{\hspace{2cm}}$

Estimate the product.

7. $5 \times 37 = \underline{\hspace{2cm}}$ 8. $715 \times 6 = \underline{\hspace{2cm}}$ 9. $178 \times 5 = \underline{\hspace{2cm}}$

10. $\$6.85 \times 3 = \underline{\hspace{2cm}}$ 11. $2{,}190 \times 7 = \underline{\hspace{2cm}}$ 12. $50 \times 58 = \underline{\hspace{2cm}}$

Multiply.

13.
$$\begin{array}{r} 23 \\ \times\ \ 3 \\ \hline \end{array}$$

14.
$$\begin{array}{r} 69 \\ \times\ \ 7 \\ \hline \end{array}$$

15.
$$\begin{array}{r} 713 \\ \times\ \ \ 3 \\ \hline \end{array}$$

16.
$$\begin{array}{r} 825 \\ \times\ \ \ 6 \\ \hline \end{array}$$

17.
$$\begin{array}{r} 509 \\ \times\ \ \ 4 \\ \hline \end{array}$$

18.
$$\begin{array}{r} 4{,}273 \\ \times\ \ \ \ 3 \\ \hline \end{array}$$

19.
$$\begin{array}{r} 6{,}035 \\ \times\ \ \ \ 7 \\ \hline \end{array}$$

20.
$$\begin{array}{r} \$5.39 \\ \times\ \ \ 8 \\ \hline \end{array}$$

21.
$$\begin{array}{r} \$23.50 \\ \times\ \ \ \ \ 9 \\ \hline \end{array}$$

22.
$$\begin{array}{r} 47 \\ \times\ 23 \\ \hline \end{array}$$

23.
$$\begin{array}{r} 74 \\ \times\ 30 \\ \hline \end{array}$$

24.
$$\begin{array}{r} 60 \\ \times\ 82 \\ \hline \end{array}$$

Bongo

© School Zone Publishing Company 02215

Circle the answer.

25. Multiply: $7 \times 900 = $ _____

   A. 630

   B. 6,300

   C. 63,000

   D. 630,000

26. Multiply: $60 \times 80 = $ _____

   A. 480

   B. 4,800

   C. 48,000

   D. 480,000

27. Estimate: 476×3 is about _____.

   A. 400×3

   B. 500×3

   C. 400×4

   D. 500×4

28. Estimate: $\$6.81 \times 8$ is about _____.

   A. $7

   B. $48

   C. $56

   D. $63

29. Multiply:

$$\begin{array}{r} 863 \\ \times\ \ 7 \\ \hline \end{array}$$

   A. 5,601   **B.** 5,621

   C. 6,021   **D.** 6,041

30. Multiply:

$$\begin{array}{r} 508 \\ \times\ \ 6 \\ \hline \end{array}$$

   A. 348   **B.** 3,048

   C. 3,448   **D.** 34,048

31. Multiply: $5,431 \times 7 = $ _____

   A. 35,017   **B.** 37,017

   C. 37,817   **D.** 38,017

32. Multiply: $78 \times 32 = $ _____

   A. 156   **B.** 390

   C. 2,396   **D.** 2,496

Dividing Two-Digit Numbers

When you divide, there are five steps to remember.
Repeat them over and over until you finish dividing.

Hummingbird

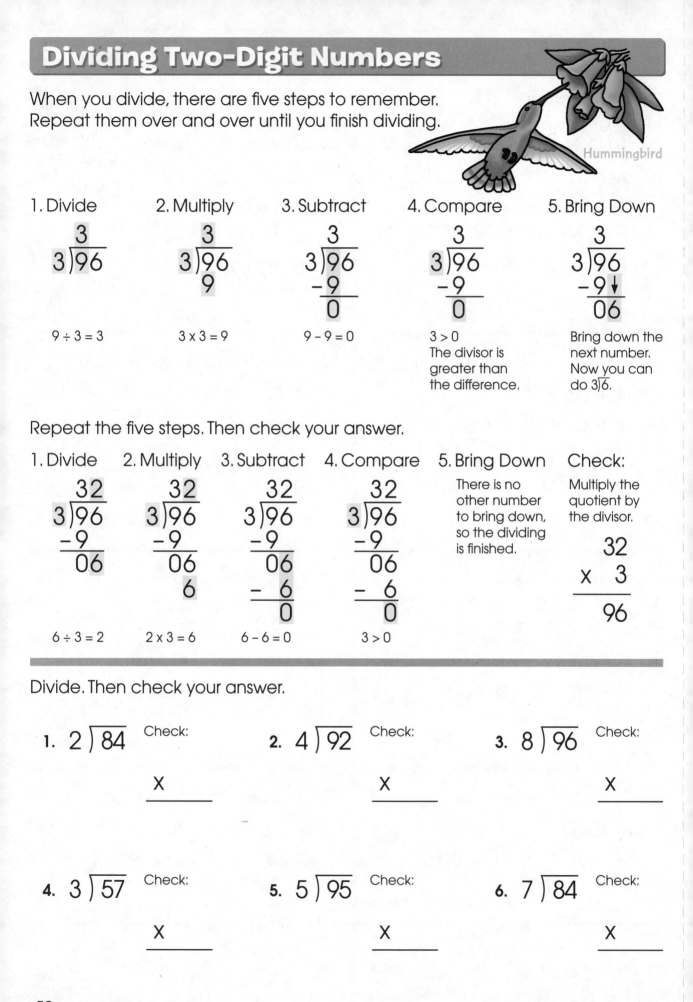

1. Divide	2. Multiply	3. Subtract	4. Compare	5. Bring Down
3 $3\overline{)96}$	3 $3\overline{)96}$ 9	3 $3\overline{)96}$ -9 0	3 $3\overline{)96}$ -9 0	3 $3\overline{)96}$ $-9\downarrow$ 06
$9 \div 3 = 3$	$3 \times 3 = 9$	$9 - 9 = 0$	$3 > 0$ The divisor is greater than the difference.	Bring down the next number. Now you can do $3\overline{)6}$.

Repeat the five steps. Then check your answer.

1. Divide	2. Multiply	3. Subtract	4. Compare	5. Bring Down	Check:
32 $3\overline{)96}$ -9 06	32 $3\overline{)96}$ -9 06 6	32 $3\overline{)96}$ -9 06 -6 0	32 $3\overline{)96}$ -9 06 -6 0	There is no other number to bring down, so the dividing is finished.	Multiply the quotient by the divisor. 32 $\times\ 3$ 96
$6 \div 3 = 2$	$2 \times 3 = 6$	$6 - 6 = 0$	$3 > 0$		

Divide. Then check your answer.

1. $2\overline{)84}$ Check:

   ___ X ___

2. $4\overline{)92}$ Check:

   ___ X ___

3. $8\overline{)96}$ Check:

   ___ X ___

4. $3\overline{)57}$ Check:

   ___ X ___

5. $5\overline{)95}$ Check:

   ___ X ___

6. $7\overline{)84}$ Check:

   ___ X ___

   © School Zone Publishing Company 02215

Estimating Quotients

To estimate a quotient, think of a basic division fact.

Think.
$48 \div 8 = 6$

Matamata Turtle

Estimate: $50 \div 8$

The estimate for $50 \div 8$ is about 6.

Estimate the quotient. Write the basic division fact under the problem. The first one is done for you.

1. $37 \div 4$ is about __9__.

   _____ $36 \div 4 = 9$ _____

2. $62 \div 8$ is about ____.

   _____

3. $26 \div 8$ is about ____.

   _____

4. $29 \div 9$ is about ____.

   _____

5. $56 \div 6$ is about ____.

   _____

6. $29 \div 5$ is about ____.

   _____

Estimate the quotient.

7. $30 \div 7$ ____

8. $40 \div 9$ ____

9. $37 \div 5$ ____

10. $29 \div 5$ ____

11. $39 \div 4$ ____

12. $52 \div 5$ ____

13. $23 \div 3$ ____

14. $58 \div 7$ ____

15. $7 \overline{)29}$

16. $6 \overline{)55}$

17. $3 \overline{)16}$

18. $8 \overline{)67}$

19. $4 \overline{)17}$

20. $4 \overline{)21}$

21. $9 \overline{)28}$

22. $5 \overline{)37}$

23. $9 \overline{)95}$

24. $4 \overline{)85}$

Quotients with Remainders

Sometimes a division problem has a **remainder**.

Tailed Jay

If 23 frogs were divided into groups of 3, there would be 7 groups of 3 and 2 frogs remaining.

The **R** stands for **remainder**.

$$\begin{array}{r} 7 \text{ R2} \\ 3\overline{)23} \\ -21 \\ \hline 2 \end{array}$$

Check: Multiply the quotient by the divisor. Then add the remainder.

$$\begin{array}{r} 7 \\ \times\ 3 \\ \hline 21 \\ +\ 2 \\ \hline 23 \end{array}$$

Divide. Then check your answer.

1. $4\overline{)47}$ Check:

2. $6\overline{)56}$ Check:

3. $5\overline{)29}$ Check:

4. $2\overline{)95}$ Check:

5. $7\overline{)89}$ Check:

6. $6\overline{)82}$ Check:

7. $4\overline{)39}$ Check:

8. $3\overline{)67}$ Check:

9. $5\overline{)52}$ Check:

© School Zone Publishing Company 02215

Dividing Three-Digit Numbers

Look closely at these two problems.

This one has a quotient with 3 digits.

This one has a quotient with 2 digits.

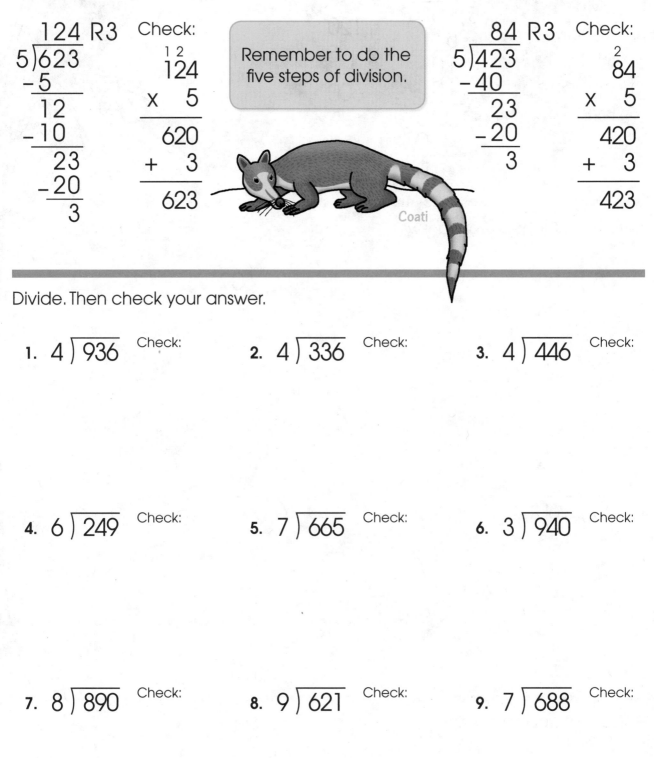

```
    124 R3      Check:
  5)623            1 2
   -5             124
   ___            x  5
    12            ____
   -10             620
   ___           +   3
    23            ____
   -20             623
   ___
     3
```

Remember to do the five steps of division.

```
     84 R3      Check:
  5)423             2
  -40              84
  ___             x  5
   23             ____
  -20              420
  ___            +   3
    3             ____
                   423
```

Coati

Divide. Then check your answer.

1. 4)936   Check:

2. 4)336   Check:

3. 4)446   Check:

4. 6)249   Check:

5. 7)665   Check:

6. 3)940   Check:

7. 8)890   Check:

8. 9)621   Check:

9. 7)688   Check:

Zeros in the Quotient

Follow the five steps for division.

1. Divide
2. Multiply
3. Subtract
4. Compare
5. Bring Down

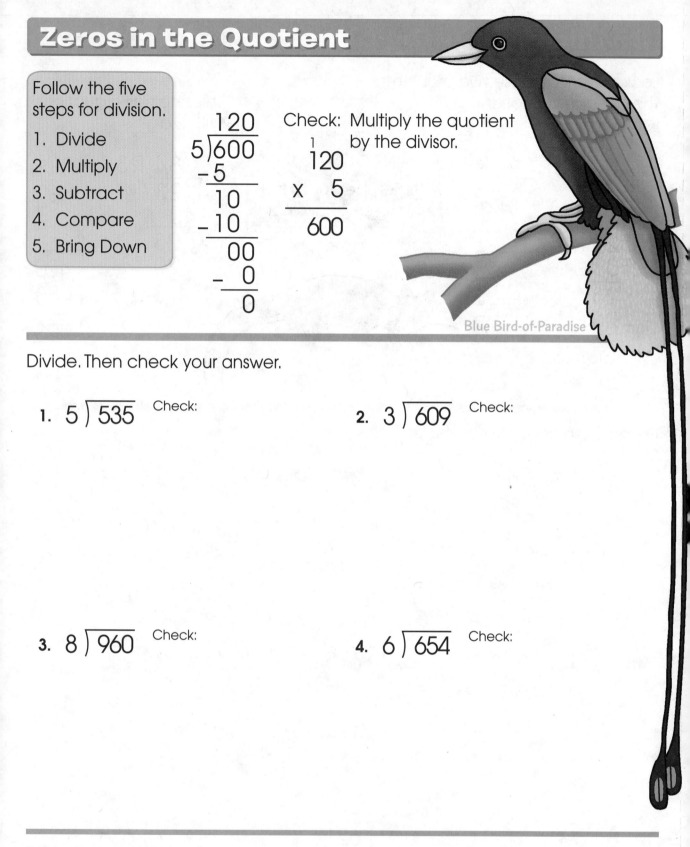

```
      120
  5)600
   -5
    10
   -10
     00
    - 0
       0
```

Check: Multiply the quotient by the divisor.

```
    1
   120
 x   5
  ────
   600
```

Blue Bird-of-Paradise

Divide. Then check your answer.

1. 5)535   Check:

2. 3)609   Check:

3. 8)960   Check:

4. 6)654   Check:

Solve the problem.

5. Joshua's family traveled 720 miles in 3 days. How many miles did they average each day? _____

© School Zone Publishing Company 02215

Division Puzzle

Divide.

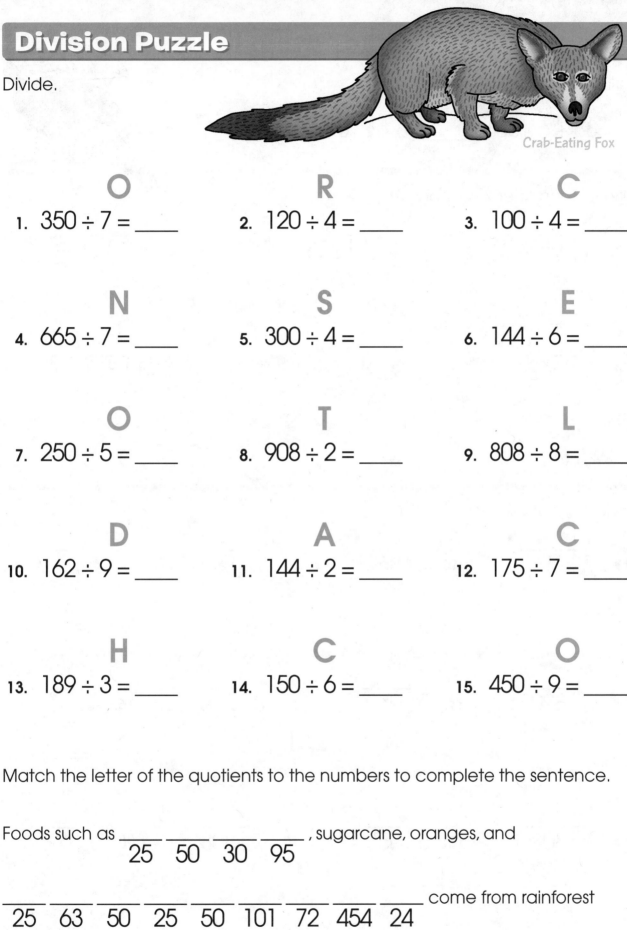

Crab-Eating Fox

O
1. $350 \div 7 =$ _____

R
2. $120 \div 4 =$ _____

C
3. $100 \div 4 =$ _____

N
4. $665 \div 7 =$ _____

S
5. $300 \div 4 =$ _____

E
6. $144 \div 6 =$ _____

O
7. $250 \div 5 =$ _____

T
8. $908 \div 2 =$ _____

L
9. $808 \div 8 =$ _____

D
10. $162 \div 9 =$ _____

A
11. $144 \div 2 =$ _____

C
12. $175 \div 7 =$ _____

H
13. $189 \div 3 =$ _____

C
14. $150 \div 6 =$ _____

O
15. $450 \div 9 =$ _____

Match the letter of the quotients to the numbers to complete the sentence.

Foods such as ____ ____ ____ ____ , sugarcane, oranges, and
          25   50   30   95

____ ____ ____ ____ ____ ____ ____ ____ ____ come from rainforest
 25 63 50 25 50 101 72 454 24

trees and plants.

What I Learned about Division

Estimate the quotient.

1. $38 \div 6$ is about _____.   2. $8 \overline{)66}$ is about _____.

Spot-Billed Toucanet

Divide. Then check your answer.

3. $4 \overline{)95}$ Check:

4. $6 \overline{)723}$ Check:

5. $8 \overline{)302}$ Check:

6. $6 \overline{)642}$ Check:

7. $4 \overline{)688}$ Check:

8. $3 \overline{)811}$ Check:

Divide. Show your work.

9. $7 \overline{)91}$

10. $4 \overline{)862}$

11. $6 \overline{)58}$

12. $5 \overline{)107}$

13. $6 \overline{)820}$

14. $5 \overline{)940}$

15. $8 \overline{)275}$

16. $4 \overline{)312}$

17. $9 \overline{)803}$

18. $6 \overline{)555}$

19. $7 \overline{)808}$

20. $3 \overline{)625}$

© School Zone Publishing Company 02215

Circle the answer.

21. Which one of the five steps is missing in order to divide numbers?

Multiply | Bring Down | Divide | Subtract

A. Add   **B.** Compare
C. Estimate   **D.** Remainder

22. How can you always check your answer to a division problem?

A. Multiply the quotient by the dividend, and then add the remainder.

B. Multiply the quotient and remainder by the divisor.

C. Multiply the quotient by the divisor.

D. Multiply the quotient by the divisor, and then add the remainder.

---

23. Estimate: $62 \div 8$ is about ____.

A. 6   **B.** 7   **C.** 8   **D.** 9

24. Estimate: $6\overline{)55}$ is about ____.

A. 7   **B.** 8   **C.** 9   **D.** 10

---

25. Divide: $916 \div 4 =$ ____

A. 219   **B.** 228 R2
C. 229   **D.** 229 R3

26. Divide: $488 \div 7 =$ ____

A. 68 R12   **B.** 69
C. 69 R5   **D.** 70 R8

---

27. Divide:
The remainder for $3\overline{)162}$ is ____.

A. 0   **B.** 3   **C.** 53   **D.** 54

28. Divide: $624 \div 3 =$ ____

A. 28   **B.** 201 R1   **C.** 208   **D.** 209

---

29. Which of these problems has a zero in the quotient?

A. $3\overline{)973}$ **B.** $3\overline{)627}$
C. $3\overline{)597}$ **D.** $3\overline{)651}$

30. Divide:
157 is the quotient for ____.

A. $4\overline{)730}$ **B.** $3\overline{)475}$
C. $5\overline{)885}$ **D.** $6\overline{)942}$

Multiplication and Division Puzzle

Work the problems out on another piece of paper. Write the answers in the puzzle.

Across

1. 346×8

5. $4\overline{)148}$

7. 2×407

8. $900 \div 6$

9. 6×0

10. 75×40

12. 9×407

13. $6\overline{)3,126}$

16. 800×3

18. 9×81

19. 107×8

Down

1. $9\overline{)252}$

2. 355×2

3. 8×8

4. $50 \times \underline{\quad} = 400$

5. $7,006 \times 5$

6. $700 \div 1$

8. $848 \div 8$

10. 4×9

11. 3×509

14. $4\overline{)968}$

15. $654 \div 6$

17. $8\overline{)368}$

Mandrills

1.	2.	3.	4.		5.	6.
7.				8.		
	9.		10.			
11.		12.				
13.	14.	15.				
16.						17.
18.				19.		

 © School Zone Publishing Company 02215

Multiplication and Division Word Problems

Giant Otter

Divide or multiply to solve the problem.

1. On Joshua's trip to South America, his family stopped to visit a rainforest. Joshua counted 58 plants in 1 square foot of the rainforest. How many plants could there be in 75 square feet of the rainforest? _____

2. Joshua's family stopped to eat at a restaurant. All 6 members of his family ate the same thing. Each person's meal cost $7.65. What was the total amount of the bill? _____

3. Before Joshua visited South America, he read a book about rainforests that had 152 pages in it. If Joshua read 8 pages each day, how many days did it take him to read the book? _____

4. Joshua took 96 snapshots of the cities he visited on his trip to share with his friends. Each of his 6 friends received the same number of snapshots. How many snapshots did each friend get? _____

Answer Key

Page 1

1. 2 + 2 = 4
   2 groups of 2 = 4
   2 x 2 = 4
2. 2 + 2 + 2 + 2 = 8
   4 groups of 2 = 8
   4 x 2 = 8
3. 3 + 3 + 3 = 9
   3 groups of 3 = 9
   3 x 3 = 9
4. 4 + 4 + 4 + 4 = 16
   4 groups of 4 = 16
   4 x 4 = 16

Page 2

1. 3 + 3 + 3 + 3 = 12
2. 5 x 3 = 15
3. 9 + 9 + 9 + 9 + 9 = 45
4. 6 x 6 = 36
5. 3 + 3 + 3 = 9
6. 2 x 8 = 16
7. 7 + 7 + 7 = 21
8. 4 x 7 = 28
9. 7 + 7 + 7 + 7 + 7 = 35
10. 5 x 9 = 45

Page 3

1. 3 x 4 = 12
2. 4 x 5 = 20
3. 5 x 2 = 10
4. 3 x 9 = 27
5. 2 x 7 = 14
6. 4 x 9 = 36

Page 4

1.	2	2.	3	3.	8, 8
	4		6	4.	18, 18
	6		9	5.	12, 12
	8		12	6.	14, 14
	10		15	7.	6, 6
	12		18		
	14		21		
	16		24		
	18		27		

Page 5

1.	4	2.	5
	8		10
	12		15
	16		20
	20		25
	24		30
	28		35
	32		40
	36		45
			5 or 0

3. 4. 5. 6. 7. 8.

Page 6

1.	0	2.	1	3. zero
	0		2	4. that number
	0		3	
	0		4	
	0		5	
	0		6	
	0		7	
	0		8	
	0		9	

Page 7

1.

x	0	1	2	3	4	5	6	7	8	9
0	0	0	0	0	0	0	0	0	0	0
1	0	1	2	3	4	5	6	7	8	9
2	0	2	4	6	8	10	12	14	16	18
3	0	3	6	9	12	15	18	21	24	27
4	0	4	8	12	16	20	24	28	32	36
5	0	5	10	15	20	25	30	35	40	45

2. 0, 2, 4, 6, 8, 10, 12, 14, 16, 18;
   0, 2, 4, 6, or 8
3. 0, 5, 10, 15, 20, 25, 30, 35, 40, 45;
   0 or 5
4. They are the column numbers.
5. 0
6. 15, 15, 6, 6; The factors are the
   same, just in a different order.

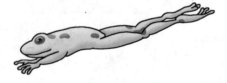

Page 8

1.	0	2.	0
	6		7
	12		14
	18		21
	24		28
	30		35
	36		42
	42		49
	48		56
	54		63

3.

7	5	35	5	8	40	3	2
3	6	18	3	1	3	2	4
21	30	42	15	8	5	6	8
7	9	63	4	6	24	9	7
8	7	56	3	48	6	4	2
7	8	49	12	54	28	36	4
7	1	7	5	35	6	0	0

Page 9

1.	0	2.	0
	8		9
	16		18
	24		27
	32		36
	40		45
	48		54
	56		63
	64		72
	72		81

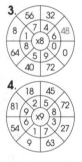

3.
4.

Page 10

42, 12, 64, 14,
40, 24, 9, 0, 21,
81, 16, 25, 42,
24, 0, 18, 16, 30,
36, 54, 9, 81, 56

Page 11

x	0	1	2	3	4	5	6	7	8	9
0	0	0	0	0	0	0	0	0	0	0
1	0	1	2	3	4	5	6	7	8	9
2	0	2	4	6	8	10	12	14	16	18
3	0	3	6	9	12	15	18	21	24	27
4	0	4	8	12	16	20	24	28	32	36
5	0	5	10	15	20	25	30	35	40	45
6	0	6	12	18	24	30	36	42	48	54
7	0	7	14	21	28	35	42	49	56	63
8	0	8	16	24	32	40	48	56	64	72
9	0	9	18	27	36	45	54	63	72	81

Page 12

1. 6	11. 36	12. 7	13. 81
2. 27	14. 40	15. 56	16. 72
3. 20	17. 15	18. 54	19. 20
4. 36	20. 32	21. 0	22. 36
5. 30			
6. 45			
7. 12			
8. 42			
9. 28			
10. 56			

Page 13

1. 4	2. 7
3. 1	4. 8
5. 4	6. 6
7. 9	8. 7
9. 2	10. 7
11. 9	12. 0
13. 0	14. 8
15. 3	16. 8

Page 14

1. 40¢; 40¢	3. 0	4. 60	5. 80
2. 100¢; 100¢	10	6. 20	7. 50
	20	8. 30	9. 90
	30	10. 10	11. 40
	40	12. 70	13. 120
	50	14. 150	15. 250
	60	16. 200	17. 320
	70	18. 500	
	80	19. 10, 0	
	90		
	100		

© School Zone Publishing Company 02215

Multiplication and Division Word Problems

Giant Otter

Divide or multiply to solve the problem.

1. On Joshua's trip to South America, his family stopped to visit a rainforest. Joshua counted 58 plants in 1 square foot of the rainforest. How many plants could there be in 75 square feet of the rainforest? _____

2. Joshua's family stopped to eat at a restaurant. All 6 members of his family ate the same thing. Each person's meal cost $7.65. What was the total amount of the bill? _____

3. Before Joshua visited South America, he read a book about rainforests that had 152 pages in it. If Joshua read 8 pages each day, how many days did it take him to read the book? _____

4. Joshua took 96 snapshots of the cities he visited on his trip to share with his friends. Each of his 6 friends received the same number of snapshots. How many snapshots did each friend get? _____

Answer Key

Page 1

1. $2 + 2 = 4$
   2 groups of 2 = 4
   $2 \times 2 = 4$
2. $2 + 2 + 2 + 2 = 8$
   4 groups of 2 = 8
   $4 \times 2 = 8$
3. $3 + 3 + 3 = 9$
   3 groups of 3 = 9
   $3 \times 3 = 9$
4. $4 + 4 + 4 + 4 = 16$
   4 groups of 4 = 16
   $4 \times 4 = 16$

Page 2

1. $3 + 3 + 3 + 3 = 12$
2. $5 \times 3 = 15$
3. $9 + 9 + 9 + 9 + 9 = 45$
4. $6 \times 6 = 36$
5. $3 + 3 + 3 = 9$
6. $2 \times 8 = 16$
7. $7 + 7 + 7 = 21$
8. $4 \times 7 = 28$
9. $7 + 7 + 7 + 7 + 7 = 35$
10. $5 \times 9 = 45$

Page 3

1. $3 \times 4 = 12$
2. $4 \times 5 = 20$
3. $5 \times 2 = 10$
4. $3 \times 9 = 27$
5. $2 \times 7 = 14$
6. $4 \times 9 = 36$

Page 4

1.	2.	3. 8, 8
2	3	3. 8, 8
4	6	4. 18, 18
6	9	5. 12, 12
8	12	6. 14, 14
10	15	7. 6, 6
12	18	
14	21	
16	24	
18	27	

Page 5

1.	2.
4	5
8	10
12	15
16	20
20	25
24	30
28	35
32	40
36	45
	5 or 0

3. 4. 5. 6. 7. 8. (dot illustrations)

Page 6

1.	2.
0	1
0	2
0	3
0	4
0	5
0	6
0	7
0	8
0	9

3. zero
4. that number

Page 7

1.

x	0	1	2	3	4	5	6	7	8	9
0	0	0	0	0	0	0	0	0	0	0
1	0	1	2	3	4	5	6	7	8	9
2	0	2	4	6	8	10	12	14	16	18
3	0	3	6	9	12	15	18	21	24	27
4	0	4	8	12	16	20	24	28	32	36
5	0	5	10	15	20	25	30	35	40	45

2. 0, 2, 4, 6, 8, 10, 12, 14, 16, 18;
   0, 2, 4, 6, or 8
3. 0, 5, 10, 15, 20, 25, 30, 35, 40, 45;
   0 or 5
4. They are the column numbers.
5. 0
6. 15, 15, 6, 6; The factors are the
   same, just in a different order.

Page 8

1.	2.
0	0
6	7
12	14
18	21
24	28
30	35
36	42
42	49
48	56
54	63

3.

7	5	35	5	8	40	3	2
3	6	18	3	1	3	2	4
21	30	42	15	8	5	6	8
7	9	63	6	4	24	9	7
8	7	56	3	48	6	4	2
7	8	49	12	54	28	36	4
7	1	7	5	35	6	0	0

Page 9

1.	2.
0	0
8	9
16	18
24	27
32	36
40	45
48	54
56	63
64	72
72	81

3.
(x8 wheel: 56, 32, 7, 4, 6, 48, 8, 3, 1, 2, 64, 5, 9, 0, 40, 72)

4.
(x9 wheel: 18, 45, 2, 5, 8, 72, 81, 9, 1, 4, 6, 3, 54, 7, 27, 9, 63)

Page 10

42, 12, 64, 14,
40, 24, 9, 0, 21,
81, 16, 25, 42,
24, 0, 18, 16, 30,
36, 54, 9, 81, 56

Page 11

x	0	1	2	3	4	5	6	7	8	9
0	0	0	0	0	0	0	0	0	0	0
1	0	1	2	3	4	5	6	7	8	9
2	0	2	4	6	8	10	12	14	16	18
3	0	3	6	9	12	15	18	21	24	27
4	0	4	8	12	16	20	24	28	32	36
5	0	5	10	15	20	25	30	35	40	45
6	0	6	12	18	24	30	36	42	48	54
7	0	7	14	21	28	35	42	49	56	63
8	0	8	16	24	32	40	48	56	64	72
9	0	9	18	27	36	45	54	63	72	81

Page 12

1. 6	11. 36	12. 7	13. 81
2. 27	14. 40	15. 56	16. 72
3. 20	17. 15	18. 54	19. 20
4. 36	20. 32	21. 0	22. 36
5. 30			
6. 45			
7. 12			
8. 42			
9. 28			
10. 56			

Page 13

1. 4	2. 7
3. 1	4. 8
5. 4	6. 6
7. 9	8. 7
9. 2	10. 7
11. 9	12. 0
13. 0	14. 8
15. 3	16. 8

Page 14

1. 40¢; 40¢
2. 100¢; 100¢

	3. 0	4. 60	5. 80
	10	6. 20	7. 50
	20	8. 30	9. 90
	30	10. 10	11. 40
	40	12. 70	13. 120
	50	14. 150	15. 250
	60	16. 200	17. 320
	70	18. 500	
	80	19. 10, 0	
	90		
	100		

© School Zone Publishing Company 02215

Answer Key

Page 15
1. 16 2. 80 3. 0
4. 90 5. 100 6. 30
7. 48 8. 40 9. 18
10. 100 11. 60 12. 81
13. 0 14. 27 15. 900

Page 16
1. 22	2. 11
33	22
44	33
55	44
66	55
77	66
88	77
99	88
110	99
121	110
132	121
	132

3. It's easy to add a 1 to the ones place and a 1 to the tens place of the previous number.

4. The numbers are doubles.

5. 0; Zero times any number equals zero.

6. 143; $10 \times 13 = 130 + 13 = 143$

Page 17
1. 24	2. 12
36	24
48	36
60	48
72	60
84	72
96	84
108	96
120	108
132	120
144	132
	144

3. even
4. 0, 2, 4, 6, or 8
5. 0; Zero times any number equals zero.
6. 84 eggs
7. 60 inches

Page 18
1. $7 + 7 + 7 + 7 = 28$
   4 groups of 7 = 28
   $4 \times 7 = 28$

2. 24   3. 6

4. 14   5. 16

6. 9   7. 36   8. 7
9. 0   10. 0   11. 24

12. 42   13. 36   14. 56
15. 64   16. 70   17. 77
18. 96   19. 100   20. 54

Page 19
21. A   22. B
23. C   24. C
25. D   26. C
27. D   28. C
29. C   30. A

Page 20
1. $12 \div 3 = 4$ 2. $8 \div 4 = 2$
   $12 \div 4 = 3$ $8 \div 2 = 4$

3. $10 \div 2 = 5$ 4. $18 \div 3 = 6$
   $10 \div 5 = 2$ $18 \div 6 = 3$

5. $12 \div 6 = 2$ 6. $20 \div 5 = 4$
   $12 \div 2 = 6$ $20 \div 4 = 5$

Page 21
1. $56 \div 8 = 7$ 2. $36 \div 4 = 9$ 3. $25 \div 5 = 5$
   $56 \div 7 = 8$ $36 \div 9 = 4$

4. $42 \div 6 = 7$ 5. $24 \div 3 = 8$ 6. $14 \div 2 = 7$
   $42 \div 7 = 6$ $24 \div 8 = 3$ $14 \div 7 = 2$

7. $35 \div 7 = 5$ 8. $72 \div 8 = 9$ 9. $32 \div 4 = 8$
   $35 \div 5 = 7$ $72 \div 9 = 8$ $32 \div 8 = 4$

10. 9 stamps

Page 22
1. 7   2. 4   3. 4

4. 1	5. 1	6. $16 \div 2 = 8$
2	2	7. $21 \div 3 = 7$ or
3	3	$21 \div 7 = 3$
4	4	8. $2 \times 9 = 18$
5	5	$18 \div 2 = 9$
6	6	9. $1 \times 3 = 3$
7	7	$3 \div 3 = 1$ or
8	8	$3 \div 1 = 3$
9	9	10. 1

Page 23
1. 5   2. 6

3. 1	4. 1	5. 3
2	2	2
3	3	8
4	4	8
5	5	1
6	6	4
7	7	9
8	8	7
9	9	1
		6

Page 24
1. 1	2. 1	3. 6
2	2	21
3	3	8
4	4	49
5	5	6
6	6	7
7	7	3
8	8	56
9	9	54

Page 25
1. 1	2. 1
2	2
3	3
4	4
5	5
6	6
7	7
8	8
9	9

3. 40, 5
   8, 5
4. 6, 54
   6, 54
5. 9, 9
   9, 9
6. 64, 8

7. $7 \times 8 = 56$
   $8 \times 7 = 56$
   $56 \div 7 = 8$
   $56 \div 8 = 7$

8. $1 \times 9 = 9$
   $9 \times 1 = 9$
   $9 \div 1 = 9$
   $9 \div 9 = 1$

9. $7 \times 9 = 63$
   $9 \times 7 = 63$
   $63 \div 7 = 9$
   $63 \div 9 = 7$

Answer Key

Page 26

1
0
7
cannot do
1
0
6
cannot do

Any number divided by 1 equals that number. 5 ÷ 1 = 5

Any non-zero number divided by itself is 1. 5 ÷ 5 = 1

Zero divided by any non-zero number equals 0. 0 ÷ 5 = 0

You cannot divide by zero. You **cannot** do 5 ÷ 0.

10
1
0
1
cannot do
0
12
1

Page 27

1. $9\overline{)36}$ → 4

2. $2\overline{)10}$ → 5

3. $8\overline{)56}$ → 7

4. $7\overline{)63}$ → 9

5. $18 \div 2 = 9$ or $18 \div 3 = 6$
   $18 \div 9 = 2$ $18 \div 6 = 3$

6. $5\overline{)30}$ → 6 or $6\overline{)30}$ → 5

7. $5\overline{)45}$ → 9 or $9\overline{)45}$ → 5

8. $54 \div 6 = 9$ or
   $54 \div 9 = 6$

9. $72 \div 9 = 8$ or
   $72 \div 8 = 9$

10. $7\overline{)7}$ → 1 or $1\overline{)7}$ → 7

11. 9   12. 7   13. 9
14. 9   15. 7   16. 9
17. 1   18. 8   19. 0

Page 28

1. $9\overline{)81}$ → 9   2. $2\overline{)8}$ → 4

3. $8\overline{)56}$ → 7   4. $7\overline{)14}$ → 2

5. 8   6. 7
7. 7   8. 10
9. 10   10. 7
11. 1   12. 8

Page 29

1. $24 \div 6 = 4$; 4 nuts
2. $3 \times 8 = 24$; 24 bananas
3. $6 \times 7 = 42$; 42 stickers
4. $9 \div 3 = 3$; 3 boats

Page 30

1. $6 \times 5 \div 3 \div 2 = 5$
2. $10 \div 5 \times 4 \div 2 = 4$
3. $49 \div 7 \times 6 \div 6 = 7$
4. $81 \div 9 \div 3 \times 6 = 18$
5. $2 \div 2 \times 2 \div 2 = 1$
   or $2 \times 2 \div 2 \div 2 = 1$
6. $64 \div 8 \div 8 \times 1 = 1$
   or $64 \div 8 \div 8 \div 1 = 1$
7. $8 \times 5 \div 4 \times 3 = 30$
8. $24 \div 8 \times 9 \div 3 = 9$

Page 31

1.4	0		2.5	6		3.3
8.8		5.2	4		6.3	6
	7.1	4		8.2	0	
9.7	2		10.1			11.6
2		12.2	8		13.2	4
	14.4	0		15.2	8	

Page 32

1. $3 \times 5 = 15$
   $15 \div 3 = 5$
2. 8   3. 9   4. 0
5. 0   6. 1   7. 0
8. $54 \div 6 = 9$ 9. $8 \div 8 = 1$ 10. $35 \div 7 = 5$
   $54 \div 9 = 6$ $8 \div 1 = 8$ $35 \div 5 = 7$
11. 8   12. 6   13. 8   14. 9
15. 9   16. 4   17. 0   18. 42
19. 1   20. 8   21. 9   22. cannot do
23. 9   24. cannot do 25. 9   26. 5

Page 33

27. B   28. C
29. C   30. D
31. D   32. C
33. B   34. D

Page 34

1. 8; 80; 800
2. 63; 630; 6,300
3. 6; 60
4. 16; 1,600
5. 27; 2,700
6. 56; 560
7. 40; 400
8. 54; 5,400
9. 700   10. 360   11. 1,500
12. 280 13. 2,400 14. 450
15. 4,200 16. 400 17. 7,200
18.

x	10	30	80	100	400	900
5	50	150	400	500	2,000	4,500
7	70	210	560	700	2,800	6,300
8	80	240	640	800	3,200	7,200

Page 35

1. $4 \times 60 = 240$ 2. $6 \times 80 = 480$ 3. $3 \times 200 = 600$
4. $600 \times 8 = 4,800$ 5. $7 \times 200 = 1,400$ 6. $5 \times 800 = 4,000$
7. 210   8. 3,200   9. 4,900
10. 2,000   11. 1,800   12. 540
13. 1,500   14. 560   15. 5,400
16. 210 photographs
17. 240 students

Page 36

1. 28   2. 48   3. 46
4. 99   5. 48   6. 77
7. 96   8. 40   9. 26
10. 36 pages

Page 37

1. 252 2. 196 3. 296 4. 102 5. 156 6. 320
7. 567 8. 54   9. 275 10. 171 11. 84 12. 225
13. 24 14. 80 15. 36

Page 38

1. 504 2. 944   3. 3,900
4. 938 5. 2,439 6. 1,152
7. 270 8. 1,460 9. 2,016

© School Zone Publishing Company 02215

Page 39
1. 312 2. 448 3. 234
4. 852 5. 1,281 6. 2,946
7. 507 8. 2,220 9. 3,660
10. 1,380 pounds
11. 6 ostriches = 2,070 pounds

Page 40
1. 903 2. 570 3. 1,950 4. 4,230
5. 2,412 6. 2,250 7. 1,530 8. 818
9. 1,428 10. 3,150 11. 3,654 12. 5,360
13. 302 x 8 = 2,416
14. 605 x 8 = 4,840
15. 340 x 5 = 1,700
16. 260 x 7 = 1,820 or 270 x 7 = 1,890

Page 41
1. 6,666 2. 15,705 3. 8,028
4. 36,856 5. 15,536 6. 15,78?
7. 21,735 8. 16,200 9. 31,75?
10. 9,000 pounds

Page 42
1. $3 x 6 = $18 2. $8 x 7 = $56 3. $40 x 3 = $120 4. $1 x 9 = $9
5. $17.58 6. $56.42 7. $127.50 8. $8.01
9. $28.50 10. $29.96 11. $114.87 12. $5.88

Page 43
1. 3 x $5.75 = $17.25
2. 6 x $1.99 = $11.94
3. 4 x $12.50 = $50.00
4. 5 x $7.09 = $35.45
5. 8 x $.65 = $5.20
6. 4 x ($7.25 + $3.89) = $44.56

Page 44
1. 600 2. 5,600 3. 3,000 4. 1,600 5. 3,600
6. 4,200 7. 4,000 8. 3,600 9. 1,200 10. 2,700
11.

x	10	20	40	50	60	80
10	100	200	400	500	600	800
30	300	600	1,200	1,500	1,800	2,400
60	600	1,200	2,400	3,000	3,600	4,800
70	700	1,400	2,800	3,500	4,200	5,600
90	900	1,800	3,600	4,500	5,400	7,200

Page 45
1. 2,387 2. 1,012 3. 1,023
4. 1,428 5. 2,332 6. 1,550
7. 276 postcards

Page 46
1. 960 2. 1,560 3. 3,150 4. 2,030
5. 620 6. 2,580 7. 1,000 8. 3,360
9. 690 10. 3,360 11. 3,550 12. 3,960
13. 900 orchids

Page 47
1. 65 x 9 = 585
2. 35 x 2 = 70
3. 653 x 9 = 5,877
4. 356 x 2 = 712
5. 6,532 x 9 = 58,788
6. 3,569 x 2 = 7,138
7. 93 x 65 = 6,045
8. 36 x 25 = 900

Page 48
1. 60 2. 350 3. 800
4. 5,600 5. 900 6. 5,400
7. 200 8. 4,200 9. 1,000
10. $21 11. 14,000 12. 3,000
13. 69 14. 483 15. 2,139 16. 4,950
17. 2,036 18. 12,819 19. 42,245 20. $43.12
21. $211.50 22. 1,081 23. 2,220 24. 4,920

Page 49
25. B 26. B
27. B 28. C
29. D 30. B
31. D 32. D

Page 50
1. 42 2. 23 3. 12
4. 19 5. 19 6. 12

Page 51
1. 9; 36 ÷ 4 = 9 2. 8; 64 ÷ 8 = 8
3. 3; 24 ÷ 8 = 3 4. 3; 27 ÷ 9 = 3
5. 9; 54 ÷ 6 = 9 6. 6; 30 ÷ 5 = 6
7. 4 8. 4 9. 7 10. 6
11. 10 12. 10 13. 8 14. 8
15. 4 16. 9 17. 5 18. 8 19. 4
20. 5 21. 3 22. 7 23. 10 or 11 24. 21

Page 52
1. 11 R3 2. 9 R2 3. 5 R4
4. 47 R1 5. 12 R5 6. 13 R4
7. 9 R3 8. 22 R1 9. 10 R2

Page 53
1. 234 2. 84 3. 111 R2
4. 41 R3 5. 95 6. 313 R1
7. 111 R2 8. 69 9. 98 R2

Page 54
1. 107 2. 203
3. 120 4. 109
5. 240 miles

Page 55
1. 50 2. 30 3. 25
4. 95 5. 75 6. 24
7. 50 8. 454 9. 101
10. 18 11. 72 12. 25
13. 63 14. 25 15. 50
corn, chocolate

Page 56
1. 6 2. 8
3. 23 R3 4. 120 R3 5. 37 R6
6. 107 7. 172 8. 270 R1
9. 13 10. 215 R2 11. 9 R4 12. 21 R2
13. 136 R4 14. 188 15. 34 R3 16. 78
17. 89 R2 18. 92 R3 19. 115 R3 20. 208 R1

Page 57
21. B 22. D
23. C 24. C
25. C 26. C
27. A 28. C
29. B 30. D

Page 58

1. 2	2. 7	3. 6	4. 8		5. 3	6. 7
7. 8	1	4		8. 1	5	0
	9. 0		10. 3	0	0	0
11. 1		12. 3	6	6	3	
13. 5	14. 2	15. 1		0		
2	4	0	0			17. 4
18. 7	2	9		19. 8	5	6

Page 59
1. 4,350 plants
2. $45.90
3. 19 days
4. 16 snapshots

CONGRATULATIONS!

_____

NAME

finished **Multiplication & Division 3-4**
from School Zone Publishing Company.